painesPLOUGH and Dundee Rep Ensemble present

dundee
Rep
THEATRE

If Destroyed True
by Douglas Maxwell

Cast (in order of appearance)

Vincent	Paul Thomas Hickey
Grace	Cora Bissett
Arlene/Mrs Young	Ann Louise Ross
Tupelo Tam/Sweeny	Robert Paterson
Michael	Keith Fleming
Ty	David Ireland
Norman	Alan Tripney

Director	John Tiffany
Designer	Neil Warmington
Lighting Designer	Natasha Chivers
Movement	Struan Leslie
Composer	Brian Docherty

Production Manager	John Miller
Technical Stage Manager	Mat Ort
Company Stage Manager	Nils den Hertog
Deputy Stage Managers	Viktoria Begg, Amy Steadman
Master Carpenter	Alex Bynoth
Assistant Carpenters	Dan Cheyne, Alan Wild
Design Assistant/Scenic Artist	Leila Kalbassi
Stage Technician	John Farmer
Chief Electrician	Richard Moffat
Head of Sound	Kinnell J Anderson
Deputy Chief Electrician	Emma Jones
Assistant Stage Managers	Lorna Adamson, Alastair Ewer
Head of Wardrobe	Phyllis Byrne
Wardrobe/Cutter	Isobel Nelms
Wardrobe Assistant	Lisa Cochrane
Wardrobe Maintenance	Irene Phillip

Press Representative	Emma Schad
	07930 308018
Cover Image	Stuart McCaffer
	lostdug@hotmail.com

First performed at Dundee Re~ ⁻

The playscript that follows w   d during rehearsal.

D1334233

DOUGLAS MAXWELL
Writer

Douglas has previously worked with Paines Plough on his play *Helmet* which was a co-production with Traverse Theatre, Edinburgh in 2002. Last year *Helmet* was translated into German and produced by the Schauspielhaus in Stuttgart. Other previous plays include *Variety* (Grid Iron/Edinburgh International Festival), *Our Bad Magnet* (Tron Theatre/ Borderline), *Decky Does A Broncho* (Grid Iron/Almeida).
Forthcoming productions include a version of Wedekind's *Spring Awakening* for Grid Iron, *Mancub* (Vanishing Point/Soho Theatre – June 2005), *Melody* (Traverse/Tron).
He is also under commission to the Traverse Theatre.

CORA BISSETT
Grace

Theatre includes: *Fierce* (Grid Iron), *Red Riding Hood* (Theatre Royal Stratford East), *Electra* (Gate), *The Breathing House*, *A Streetcar Named Desire*, *Miseryguts*, *Beauty and the Beast*, *The Comedy of Errors* (Royal Lyceum Edinburgh), *Caledonian Road* (Almeida), *Sunset Song* (Prime Productions), *Red* (Boilerhouse), *Horses, Horses Coming in All Directions*, *I Licked a Slags Deodorant* (Arches Theatre), *Citizone* (Headspace Productions), *Dr Faustus* (TAG), *Speed Run* (Tron Theatre). TV includes: *Casualty* (BBC), *High Times*, *Taggart* (SMG). Film includes: *Travelling Light* (Short – Edinburgh Art College), *Saved* (Short – Cormorrant Films), *Pasty Faces* (Noel Gay Motion Pictures), *The Tragic History of Jackson Pollock* (Athens Films). Radio includes: *The Zeitgeist Man* (Radio 4). Cora has written and released two albums with her own bands Darlingheart and Swelling Meg.

BRIAN DOCHERTY
Composer

The main protagonist behind Scientific Support Dept and Serf, Brian has produced and collaborated with: Adventures in Stereo, Alan Vega [Suicide], Cowboy Mouth, Karen Matheson, Daddy's Favorite, Nectarine no.9, Gareth Seger, Shara Nelson, Sugartown, The McCluskey Brothers, Del Amitri, Babygod, James Grant and Love and Money, This Mortal Coil. Theatre works include: *Othello*, *Stroma* (TAG Theatre Company), *Macbeth* (Awarehaus Theatre), *Among Unbroken Hearts* (Traverse Theatre), *Helmet* (Traverse Theatre and Paines Plough), *Brazil* (Theatre of Imagination), *The Danny Crowe Show* (Dundee Rep), *The Doll Tower* (Liverpool Unity Theatre in collaboration with Liverpool Philharmonic Orchestra). As short film and music video-director: The Far Lows – Scientific Support Dept, Machin Truc – babygod, Hopper – Serf.

KEITH FLEMING
Michael

Keith trained at Chelsea Art College and the Guildhall School of Music and Drama.
For Dundee Rep Ensemble: *The Visit*, *Merlin the Magnificent*, *A Lie Of The Mind*, *Macbeth*, *Scenes from an Execution*, *Dumbstruck!*, *Peter Pan*, *Rum and Vodka*, *The Danny Crowe Show*, *Twelfth Night*, *The Laird O'Grippy*, *Dancing at Lughnasa*, *The Snow Queen*, *The Night Before Christmas*, *The Censor*, *The Duchess of Malfi*, *Nightflights*, *Pants*, *Measure for Measure*, *Puss in Boots*, *A'body's Aberdee*, *The Seagull*, *Mince?*, *Cabaret*, *The Winter's Tale*, *The Land of Cakes* and *A Midsummer Night's Dream*. Other theatre includes: *A Clockwork Orange* (International Tour), *Room* (Edinburgh Festival), *Peter Pan*, *A Great Reckonin'* (Perth Theatre). TV includes *Split Second* (Screen One, BBC), *Monarch of the Glen* (BBC/Ecosse), *Crimewatch* (BBC). Film includes: *Kings of the Wild Frontier* (Scottish Screen) and *Halloween 3D*.

PAUL THOMAS HICKEY
Vincent

For Paines Plough: *Crave*. Other theatre includes: *Slab Boys Trilogy*, *Gagarin Way*, *Green Field*, *Olga*, *Passing Places*, *The Architect* (Traverse), *San Diego* (Tron), *The Entertainer* (Citizens), *AD*, *Macbeth*, *Ecstasy*, *One Flew Over the Cuckoos Nest*, *Still Life*, *Wasted* (Raindog Ltd), *The Backroom* (Bush/Soho), *Mainstream*, *Timeless* (Suspect Culture), *Snatch* (Soho Theatre), *Shining Souls* (Old Vic), *Slab Boys Trilogy* (Young Vic), *Jump the Life to Come*, *A Night of Gentle Sex Comedies* (7:84), *Sailmaker*, *Twelfth Night* (TAG), *Merlin* (Cumbernauld Theatre). TV includes: *Tinsel Town* (BBC Scotland), *Nightlife*, *Cardiac Arrest*, *The Jacobites*, *Sweetest Feeling* (BBC), *Taggart*, *The High Road*, *Britoil Fraud* (STV). Film includes: *California Sunshine*, *Wanting and Getting* (Zigma Films), *Charmed* (EVTC), *Lay of the Land* (BFI/FilmFour Lab). Radio includes: *L'assommoir* (BBC Radio 4).

DAVID IRELAND
Ty

David is an associate Member of Dundee Rep Ensemble. He trained at the Royal Scottish Academy of Music and Drama. For Dundee Rep Ensemble: *The Visit*, *Merlin the Magnificent* and *A Lie of the Mind*. Theatre includes: *Macbeth*, *Revenge* (Tinderbox), *Soul Pilots* (Ek Performance), *The Lieutenant of Inishmore* (RSC), *Lament* (Suspect Culture), *Factory Girls* (7:84), *Variety* (Grid Iron/Edinburgh International Festival), *Decky Does a Bronco* (Grid Iron/Almeida), *Swimming* (Arches, Glasgow), *Observe the Sons of Ulster Marching Towards the Somme* (Citizens, Glasgow), *The Sightless* (Vanishing Point), *Stroma* (TAG), *Romeo and Juliet* (Lyceum, Edinburgh) and *King Lear* (Royal Exchange, Manchester). TV includes: *Real Men* (BBC).

STRUAN LESLIE
Movement

Born in Dundee and started dancing and choreographing there with Royston Maldoom. Training includes; London Contemporary Dance School, The Naropa Institute, Boulder, Colorado. Movement direction and choreography includes: *Fix-Up*, *Iphigenia At Aulis*, *Ivanov*, Ted Hughes' version of *The Oresteia* (National Theatre), *Oliver Twist*, (Lyric Theatre Hammersmith and National Tour), *Slab Boys Trilogy*, *Solemn Mass For A Full Moon in Summer* (Traverse Edinburgh also Bite at Barbican, London), *The Girl Of Sand* (Almeida Opera), *Jephtha* (Welsh National Opera and English National Opera), *Jenufa*, *Cosi Fan Tutte* (Welsh National Opera), *Katya Kabanova* (Geneva and WNO), *Attempts On Her Life* (Teatro Piccolo, Milan), *A Midsummer Night's Dream* (Regent's Park), *Iphigenia At Aulis* (Abbey Theatre), *The Maids*, *Julius Caesar* (Young Vic/Japanese tour also as actor), *The Country*, *Forty Winks* (Royal Court), *Endgame* (Donmar Warehouse), *Antigone* (TAG), *As You Like It*, *Cyrano De Bergerac*, *Easter*, *Slaughter City*, *Merchant Of Venice*, *Duchess of Malfi* (Royal Shakespeare Company), *Easy Virtue* (Chichester). Televison includes: choreography for *Casanova* (BBC/Red productions), *Little Dorrit* (BBC), *Out On Tuesday* (Alfalfa Productions/ Channel 4). Directing work includes: *The Snow Queen* (GSA Conservatoire), *Love Lust and Loss* (BAC), *The Holy Whore and Newchild Trilogy* (devised pieces for his own ensemble thewatercompany), *Mourning Becomes Electra*, *Serious Money* (ArtsEd London), *Opera Cuts Carmen* (WNO), *10,000 Broken Mirrors*, *Spinning* (Oval House). Struan is co-Artistic Director, with composer Simon Deacon, of Next Generation, a music collaboration development project funded by Youth Music at the National Theatre based in SE London. He also regularly teaches and leads workshops with dancers, actors and singers for organisations such as the Laban Centre London, Young Vic

Theatre and Glyndebourne Opera as well as all the main drama schools. He has also held posts at the universities of Greenwich and South Bank in London, and Illinois at Urbana Champaign, USA where he was visiting professor in the faculty of Applied Arts.

ROBERT PATERSON
Tupelo Tam/Sweeny

Robert trained at University of Glasgow and Drama Studio, London. For Dundee Rep Ensemble: *The Visit*, *Macbeth*, *Scenes from an Execution*, *Dumbstruck!*, *Peter Pan*, *The Danny Crowe Show*, *Twelfth Night*, *The Laird O'Grippy*, *The Winter's Tale*, *The Snow Queen*, *The Mill Lavvies*, *The Duchess of Malfi*, *Nightflights*, *Pants*, *Mince?*, *Measure for Measure*, *STIFF!*. Other theatre includes: *Woyzeck*, *Glengarry Glen Ross*, *The Comedy of Errors* and *Beauty and the Beast* (Royal Lyceum, Edinburgh); *A Midsummer Night's Dream* (Brunton Theatre, Musselburgh). TV includes: *Last Legs*, *Sword of Honour*, *Rebus*. Film includes: *Braveheart*. As a writer he has had plays commissioned by Radio 4 and by several theatres. A production of his adaptation of R L Stevenson's *Kidnapped* toured Scotland as did his adaptation of *Jekyll and Hyde* with Alasdair McCrone. He is Associate Director at Mull Theatre where he has directed *The Beauty Queen of Leenane*, *The Woman in Black* and *Skylight*. He also directed Dundee Rep's recent Christmas show *Merlin the Magnificent*.

ANN LOUISE ROSS
Arlene /Mrs Young

For Dundee Rep Ensemble: *The Visit*, *Merlin the Magnificent*, *A Lie Of The Mind*, *Macbeth*, *Scenes from an Execution*, *Dumbstruck!*, *Flora, the Red Menace*, *Twelfth Night*, *The Laird O'Grippy*, *The Duchess of Malfi*, *Nightflights*, *Pants*, *A'body's Aberdee*, *The Seagull*, *Mince?*, *The Winter's Tale*, *Lambrusco Nights*, *Hansel and Gretel*, *Plague*, *Cabaret*, *All My Sons*, *The Princess and the Goblin*, *A Family Affair*, *A Midsummer Night's Dream*. Other theatre includes: *The Glass Menagerie* (Byre Theatre, St. Andrews), *The Snow Queen*, *Britannia Rules*, *Juno and the Paycock*, *The Maiden Stone* and *The Steamie* (Royal Lyceum, Edinburgh), *Greta*, *Widows* and *Bondagers* (Traverse Theatre), *When I was a Girl I Used to Scream and Shout* (Brunton Theatre), *Earthquake Weather* (Starving Artists), *Plaza* (Tron Theatre), *Who's Afraid of Virginia Woolf?* (Dundee Rep). Film and TV credits include: *Trainspotting*, *Acid House Trilogy*, *Split Second* (Stockbridge Films) *Patsy Payne's Dream Machine* (C4) *Life Support*, *Looking After Jo Jo*, *Hamish Macbeth* and *The Key* (BBC), *Drifting* (TT02), *Horsehair* (Prime Cuts Short), and *The Witch's Daughter* (STV), plus numerous radio broadcasts.

JOHN TIFFANY
Director

John trained at Glasgow University and has been Associate Director at Paines Plough since 2001. Previously he was Literary Director at the Traverse. For Paines Plough: *Mercury Fur*, *The Straits* (Pearson Best Play, Herald Angel for Directing Excellence), *Helmet* (Manchester Evening News Nomination for Best Production). Other theatre includes: *The Entertainer* (Liverpool Playhouse), *Playhouse Creatures* (West Yorkshire Playhouse), *Falling* (Bush), *Gagarin Way* (Traverse/ National Theatre – First Of The Firsts, Herald Angel, Scotsman's Readers'Poll Awards and Olivier Award Nomination), *Among Unbroken Hearts* (Traverse/ Bush), *Abandonment*, *King Of The Fields*, *The Juju Girl*, *Danny 306 +Me (4 Ever)* (Traverse/Birmingham Rep), *Perfect Days* (Traverse/Hampstead – Fringe First and Oliver Award Nomination), *Greta* (Traverse) and *Passing Places* (Traverse). Film includes: *Karmic Mothers* by Kate Atkinson (BBC Tartan Shorts) and *Golden Wedding* by Andrea Gibb (BBC Two Lives – MHM Award for Best Drama).

This is John's last production for Paines Plough before he joins the new National Theatre of Scotland as Associate Director (New Work).

ALAN TRIPNEY
Norman

Alan trained at RSAMD. Theatre includes: *Cutting a Rug*, *The Slab Boys* (Traverse Theatre), *The Chrysalids* (Complete Productions), *The Twits*, *Scrooge* (Citizens Theatre), *UN*, *Savage*, *Lord of the Flies* (Raindog), *The Don*, *Brutopia*, *The Hypochondriac*, *The War of the Roses*, *Prometheus Bound*, *The Mountain Giants*, *Attempts on her Life* (RSAMD). TV includes: *Monarch of the Glen* (BBC/Ecosse).

NEIL WARMINGTON
Designer

Neil graduated in Fine Art Painting from Maidstone College of Art before attending the Motley theatre design course in London. Neil is designing *The Small Things*, *Pyrenees* and *If Destroyed True* in our This Other England season. For Paines Plough: *The Straits*, *The Drowned World*, *Splendour*, *Riddance*, *Crazy Horse*. Other theatre includes: *King Lear* (ETT/Old Vic), *Ghosts*, *Don Juan*, *John Gabriel Borkman*, *Taming of the Shrew*, *Love's Labour's Lost* (ETT), *Woyzeck*, *The Glass Menagerie*, *Comedians*, *Tankred Dorsts Merlin* (Royal Lyceum Edinburgh), *Full Moon For A Solemn Mass*, *Family*, *Passing Places*, *King of the Fields*, *Gagarin Way* (also National Theatre), *Slab Boys Trilogy* (Traverse), *Angels in America* (7:84), *Life's a Dream*, *Fiddler on the Roof*, *Playhouse Creatures* (West Yorkshire Playhouse), *Henry V* (RSC), *Much Ado About Nothing* (Queen's London), *Sunset Song*, *Mary Queen of Scots Got Her Head Chopped Off* (Theatre Royal, Glasgow), *The Life of Stuff* (Donmar), *Waiting for Godot* (Liverpool Everyman), *The Tempest* (Contact), *Jane Eyre*, *Desire Under the Elms* (Shared Experience), *Troilus & Cressida* (Opera North), *Oedipus Rex* (Connecticut State Opera), *The Marriage of Figaro* (Garsington Opera), *Scenes From An Execution*, *Dumbstruck*, *Lie Of The Mind* (Dundee), *Knives in Hens*, *The Birthday Party* (TAG). Neil has also won three TMA Awards for best design, been part of numerous Edinburgh Fringe First productions and has been awarded The Linbury Prize for stage design, and the Sir Alfred Munnings Florence Prize for painting.

PAINES PLOUGH'S THIS OTHER ENGLAND

at the Menier Chocolate Factory
Friday 28 January – Sunday 22 May 2005.

"If new writing in this country is going to have any far-reaching significance, then it needs Paines Plough"
THE INDEPENDENT

This Other England is a ground-breaking body of work marking the 30th anniversary of new writing powerhouse Paines Plough.

Taking its cue from Melvyn Bragg's BBC Radio 4 series The Routes of English, Paines Plough commissioned eight outstanding voices of theatre to think about English as a language and how it shapes our identity. This season we premiere the first four of these commissions which offer a theatrical cross-section of where we are now. This is the start of an extraordinary series, we hope you will join us and be a part of it from the beginning.

"Paines Plough remains at the Pinnacle of New British theatre." METRO

An exceptional season deserves a great venue and we are proud to be presenting these productions at London's most inspiring new venue – the Menier Chocolate Factory – which offers a unique space minutes from London Bridge with an atmospheric bar and delicious candlelit restaurant.

This season would not have been possible without the vision and commitment of our co-producing partners. For Mercury Fur; Drum Theatre Plymouth. For Pyrenees; Tron Theatre Glasgow and in association with Watford Palace Theatre. For If Destroyed True; Dundee Rep Theatre. Each production is appearing at its associated venue as well as in London during the season.

THE SMALL THINGS by Enda Walsh
Menier Chocolate Factory, London. Fri 28 Jan – Sun 27 Feb.
MERCURY FUR by Philip Ridley
Drum Theatre Plymouth. Thurs 10 Feb – Sat 26 Feb.
Menier Chocolate Factory, London. Tues 1 Mar – Sun 27 Mar.
PYRENEES by David Greig
Tron Theatre, Glasgow. Wed 9 Mar – Sat 26 Mar.
Menier Chocolate Factory, London. Tues 29 Mar – Sun 24 Apr.
Watford Palace Theatre. Tues 26 Apr – Sat 30 Apr.
IF DESTROYED TRUE by Douglas Maxwell
Dundee Rep Theatre. Sat 9 Apr – Sat 23 Apr.
Menier Chocolate Factory, London. Tues 26 Apr – Sun 22 May.

Supported by the Peggy Ramsay Foundation

PAINES PLOUGH PRESENTS... ENGAGE

Engage: Take part, participate, involve (a person or his or her attention), intensely, employ (a person), begin a battle with, bring (a mechanism) into operation.

engage: Wild Lunch Funsize

Paines Plough and Half Moon YoungPeople's Theatre are developing short plays for little people by grown up writers – Jennifer Farmer, Dennis Kelly, Abi Morgan, Chloe Moss, Gary Owen and Mark Ravenhill. Performances will be at lunchtime on Tues 22 Mar, Wed 23 Mar, Thurs 24 Mar, Thurs 31 Mar, Fri 1 April and Sat 2 April. Find a child under 7 and bring them along. Tickets are available from Half Moon on 020 7709 8900 and tickets@halfmoon.org.uk.

engage: Battle

Chaired by Michael Billington. Leading playwrights duel with each other to persuade the audience that their chosen dramatist is the greatest of all time. You decide who wins. Battle commences at 6.30pm on Fri 4 Mar and Fri 29 April. [FREE]

engage: Later

Curated by Mark Ravenhill. A series of surprising, late night theatrical events dotted throughout the season. Mark will be taking his pick of performers and artists and presenting a taste of their latest work. Performances will be post-show on Fri 25 Feb, Fri 25 Mar, Fri 22 Apr and Fri 20 May. [FREE]

engage: Explore

A chance to take a look behind-the-scenes of This Other England – come down to the Chocolate Factory. We will be receiving visitors from 11am – 3pm on Wed 9 Feb and Wed 6 April [FREE]

engage: Discuss

Each post show discussion will feature a contribution from a guest expert. [FREE]

The Small Things	I speak therefore I am	Thurs 17 Feb
Mercury Fur	When Words Lose Meaning	Thurs 17 Mar
Pyrenees	Language and Identity	Thurs 14 Apr
If Destroyed True	Language and Technology	Thurs 12 May

engage: Whispers of Britain

Assistant Director Hamish Pirie in a dynamic theatrical lecture recounts his pilgrimage to take a Chinese whisper around the British Isles. Performances will be at lunchtimes on Thurs 12 and Fri 13 May. [FREE]

engage: Masterclasses

A new series of our successful writers masterclasses will take place during the second half of This Other England. Full details of dates, titles and workshop leaders will be available at the start of the season.

engage: Schools

We will be offering a limited number of workshops for schools to accompany each of the productions. If you would like to find out more about our provision for schools please contact Susannah on 020 72404533.

Free events are not ticketed and seating is limited so please arrive at the venue in plenty of time to ensure your place.

More information on the participants and content of these events will be available nearer to the time. If you would like to be the first to find out more please email Susannah@painesplough.com with 'e-ngage' in the subject line.

PAINES PLOUGH

"The legendary Paines Plough" INDEPENDENT

Paines Plough is an award-winning nationally and internationally renowned touring theatre company, specialising exclusively in the commissioning and development of contemporary playwrights and the production of their work on stage. We tour the work throughout Britain and overseas ensuring the widest possible audience can benefit from it.

We work with both new and experienced writers and develop plays with a ground-breaking and highly respected programme of workshops and readings. In order to inspire new playwrights and find new audiences, we also have a pioneering education and outreach programme which focuses on encouraging people to write.

Our writers are encouraged to be courageous in their work, to challenge our notions of theatre and the society we live in.

Paines Plough was founded in 1974 by director John Adams and playwright David Pownall to commission and tour new plays. At the time it was the only such company in England and quickly became known as The Writers Company, for its commitment to placing the writer at the centre of the company.

Although Paines Plough has changed direction with the vision of each Artistic Director, there has always been a consistency in commissioning the best writers of each generation and touring this work nationally. These include David Pownall, Stephen Jeffreys, Heathcote Williams, Terry Johnson, Tony Marchant, Pam Gems, Mark Ravenhill, Sarah Kane, Abi Morgan, Gary Owen, David Greig, Philip Ridley, Douglas Maxwell, Enda Walsh, Gregory Burke. Many of these writers have received subsequent commissions from national and regional theatres, film and television companies here and abroad.

At the end of 2004 Paines Plough appointed its eighth Artistic Director, Roxana Silbert, she joins the company in January 2005 ready to lead us into our next exciting phase.

If you would like to be on Paines Plough's free mailing list, please send your details to:

Helen Poole
Paines Plough, 4th Floor, 43 Aldwych, LONDON WC2B 4DN
T + 44 (0) 20 7240 4533
F + 44 (0) 20 7240 4534
office@painesplough.com
www.painesplough.com

Paines Plough is supported by:

ARTS COUNCIL
ENGLAND

Paines Plough would like to thank the following, without whom This Other England would not have been possible:

Alan Brodie
Robert Kent & Blinkhorns
Casarotto Ramsay
Carolyn Bonnyman
Tricia Mahoney
David James
The Agency
Robbie Jarvis
Ashley Pharoah
Kim Oliver
Ann Bowen
Alan Ayckbourn
Adam Kenwright Associates

Tamara Cizeika
Nick Eliott
Joachim Fleury
Alison Richie
A D Penalver
Kacey Ainsworth
David Aukin and Nancy Meckler
Sheila Reid
Antoine Dupuy D'Angeal
David Bradshaw
Miranda Sawyer
Trudi Styler
Old Vic New Voices

DUNDEE REP THEATRE

"The most exciting…the most consistently interesting – arguably the best theatre in Scotland." THE SCOTSMAN

Based at the heart of the city's cultural quarter, Dundee Rep is a unique organisation in the UK, providing one of the most comprehensive arts services in Scotland. It is a thriving artistic community made up of 3 major elements:

• Dundee Rep Ensemble – the only full-time company of actors in Scotland.
• Scotland's principal contemporary dance company – Scottish Dance Theatre.
• A hugely successful and far-reaching Education & Community team.

The Rep has two artistic directors – James Brining and Dominic Hill. Under their leadership, the theatre produces a repertoire of acclaimed work. The Rep also commissions the best playwrights to create new works and translate and adapt classical texts, making it relevant to Scotland's contemporary cultural and social climate.

Over recent years the Rep has taken its place as Scotland's major producing theatre, gaining both public and critical acclaim.
Achievements include:

• Opening its doors in September 1999 to one of the most ambitious experiments in Scottish Theatre for many years – a permanent company of actors.
• In 2004, receiving 10 nominations and winning 5 Critics Awards for Theatre in Scotland.
• A Critics' Circle National Dance Award to Scottish Dance Theatre for Outstanding Company Repertoire 2003.

The 455-seat auditorium boasts one of the best stages in Scotland in terms of relationship with the audience. It operates as both a producing house – staging at least six of its own productions each year, and a receiving house – hosting work from the best visiting companies throughout Scotland and the UK. This enables the Rep to provide a wide variety of work including top quality drama, musicals, contemporary & classical dance, children's theatre, jazz, opera and more …

Dundee Rep aims to build on its many successes and plans to take the theatre and its ensemble company forward to an even more exciting future.

Artistic Director/Chief Executive	James Brining
Executive Director	Lorna Duguid
Artistic Director	Dominic Hill
Associate Director Education & Community	Steven Small
Artistic Director Scottish Dance Theatre	Janet Smith
Production Manager	John Miller
Head of Marketing	Nicola Young
Press & Publicity Manager	Drew Tosh

Dundee Rep, Tay Square, Dundee DD1 1PB
01382 227684
www.dundeerep.co.uk

IF DESTROYED TRUE

First published in 2005 by Oberon Books Ltd
521 Caledonian Road, London N7 9RH
Tel: 020 7607 3637 / Fax: 020 7607 3629
e-mail: oberon.books@btconnect.com
www.oberonbooks.com

A catalogue record for this book is available from the British
Library.

ISBN: 1 84002 563 8

Photograph by Stuart McCaffer (lostdug@hotmail.com)

Printed in Great Britain by Antony Rowe Ltd, Chippenham

ta toom   ta toom   ta too

ta toom   ta toom   ta toon

>:GREETINGS FROM NEW FLOOD.........

toom   ta toom   ta toom

TA

TOOM

>:*I wish I could make someone really happy.*

Vincent   There's two sides to every story, so they say.
             Sounds about right.
             And after tonight, listening to a whole town talk and
             watching the balloons going up,
             I reckon I know everything there is to know about
             this sorry little tale.
             Not only that, but in a way, I *am* the story.
             I'm the happy ending and all the shit that came before
             it.
             Both sides.
             Part destroyed
             Part not.
             So yes
             I'm the perfect little geezer for this nasty little job.

             So here goes.

             Two interesting things have happened in my life.

             The first happened BEFORE.

             Before New Flood was named the worst town in
             Scotland and given all that dough.
             Before I came up with THE BIG IDEA to make it
             worse.
             Before Ty's demise and Sweeny's rise.
             Before the Dylan thing and Network Flood.
             Before my Gran fucked off.
             Before the blood graffiti that spelt true love.
             Before all of that.

             Here, this takes me back.   29 years to be precise.
             Tupelo Tam was still alive and so was my mum.
             I was still tucked up tight in her tum.

Before I was broken down my right hand side and
completely fucked up for the rest of my life.
Before that.
Just.

Ten minutes before that.

There she is.
There's us.

The closest thing New Flood has to a high rise and
we're high inside it.
Top floor.
She's off her face and on the blower.
I'm in there. Inside her.
Listen to the tom-tom of my tiny heart.
T-Toom. T-Toom.
I was alright when I was in that womb.

But silly mummy's been under some strain.
My much anticipated debut is only weeks away.
So she's done the only sensible thing
And taken a massive heroin overdose.
Deliberate you ask?
We'll see. We'll see.

She's on the phone to *her* mum.
Funny how mothers come back into play when the
end of life is moments away.
Arlene, her mum, my Gran, is in a wee white house
ten minutes away.
At this precise moment, everything is ten minutes
away.

Arlene was thinking about how different her life
would have been,
Had her mother told her to take risks.
But now look where she is.

Tupelo Tam, her man, the father of all of this, doesn't budge when the phone rings.
Apart from the essentials he hasn't moved unnecessarily for years.
His chair is a body-mould, facing the TV, away from the horror of that pictureless wall.
He's hardly thought about Bob Dylan at all. Hardly at all.

>:*I wish I could make someone really happy.*

TOOM TTOOM TTOOM...

Arlene   I'm getting that am I?

Tupelo Tam   mmmmmmmmmmmm

Vincent   Arlene knew from the hiss on the line   sh
                                                             sh
                                                             sh
                                                             sh
                                                             sh
                                                             sh

              that this would be the last time she spoke to her daughter.
              She knew this, by the hiss on the line.

Grace   mooooam ma ma .shit………ma

Arlene   Is it you? Oh God. What is it hen? Are you…what is it?

Grace   mam'm…sorry……mum. I'm…away…

Arlene   Grace doll. I……don't know what to do.

                              Vincent
                                    Poor Gran.

Arlene	What do I do?

                        Vincent
                            Arlene knew that she'd
                            never been helpful.
                            Never grabbed her
                            children as they were
                            about to fall. She didn't
                            know what to do at all.

Arlene	Just… say……cheerio.
Grace	Cheee. Bye……bye mum.
Arlene	Bye bye.
Grace	Bye
Arlene	Bye darling…I'm sorry.
Grace	Bye bye mum.
Arlene	B…Bye bye my…baby. Bye bye my beautiful baby. Bye b

sssssssssssssssssssssssssssssssssssssssssssssssssssssssshhhhhhhhhhhhhhhhhhhhhhhhhhhhhhhhhhhhh

Vincent	When she turned and looked Tam in the eye
	Tam knew too. Knew his daughter's life was nearly over.
	Christ, there's knowledge DNA will never uncover.
	Tupelo Tam slowly rose from his seat.
	Like a shipwreck dredged from the bottom of the sea.
	They hadn't really spoken in years
	Words were beginnings that would end in tears for Tam and Arlene.
	But he knew what he had to do.
	Tupelo Tam
	Ran.

Vincent   Heart screeching stomach heaving legs ripping
             corroded tendons lolling off-centre gut churning fists
             panicking head boiling
             Oh my God! Tam is running!
             Charging towards his daughter.
             The song is in his head for the first time in years.
             And it strikes him

Tam   I'm her father!

Vincent   He remembers her asking

Grace   Why do bad things happen?

Vincent   When they were sharing crisps on a towel on a beach
             And wanting to hold her, his wee girl.
             Maybe kill her, just to save her, from the backstreets
             of the world.
             He remembered the first time she said

Grace   I hate you.

Vincent   And the first time he hated her too.
             He remembered the policeman that came knocking

Tam   There's real criminals out there you should be
             harassing.

Vincent   And the exhaustion that started then and has never
             really lifted.
             Until now.
             Now

Tam   I'm her father!

Vincent   Mummy dearest is at the window, gasping for air.
             Is she already blacking out?

Already losing balance?
How on earth is she staying conscious?
Did her unborn child get spared a thought?
No.
Apparently not.
Tam calls out for

Tam	Grace!
Vincent	But Grace can't see him.
Grace	Daddy?
Vincent	Her Daddy will save her. If only he could see her. So she stumbles up the stairs to the roof. And she stands on tip toes, on the ledge. I know, I know, it doesn't make sense, but that's what she did. And that's when she slid.

Tam's heart's a siren.
Toxic booms that poison, deafen

TOOMTTOOMTTOOMTTOOMTTOOMT

It's screaming out

>:*Stop! Stop!*

And then it did.
His heart imploded when he saw his daughter slip and fall eight floors

ttoom

ttoom

t
sh
sh
sh
sh
sh

We are, all of us, falling.

Grace died. Smashed into concrete
Tam died. Burst in the chest and twisted.
At the very same instant.
On the very same ground.

You might say, she broke my fall.
Incredible that I survived at all.
You might say
But I was a wish in a burst balloon.

ttoom ttoom ttoom ttoo

My heartbeat, like a satellite sound, emerged, from
behind the moon

>:*He's lucky to be alive*
They told Arlene in the hospital
But she didn't think so.
I was born broken.
Never to survive this world of perfection.

Part destroyed,
Part not.

But here's my belief.
And it runs right through the centre of this
Like the name of a town through a stick of rock.

I believe that as they fell

Tupelo Tam and my lonesome Mum
As they fell, their eyes met.

Dot dot dot dot
Dot dot dot

And when they joined, these dots

This father
This daughter

Time froze.
And sins were forgotten.
Promises kept.
When their eyes met
Everything that had happened in their heartbroken
lives
For once
Felt
True.

If Destroyed True (If Not Destroyed True)

by

Douglas Maxwell

PART ONE   IF DESTROYED TRUE...

Vincent   This is my bench.
I didn't build it or anything, they have stoned sixteen
year olds in council boots for that.

There's a plaque at the back

> *>: For Tam and his beloved daughter Grace.*
> *"Forever Young".*

Gran's idea.
Next to the plaque someone's written in green felt tip

> *>: Janice Connelly gets blow jobs from her dog.*

Intriguing I admit,
But not the most important piece of graffiti in this
story by a long, long chalk.

Nearly thirty years have come and gone.
And I've been coming and going here for so long,
with my carry out and letters that it seems almost
normal.

I am surrounded on all sides by the tiny town of New
Flood.

How did it come to this?
Where are the happy paddlers of yesteryear?
Where are the rose gardens from the postcard days?
Where are the postcards?

I dunno. But no-one's to blame.

No-one was upset when the community centre closed.
No-one read the final issue of the local paper.
No-one prayed when the last Mass was said to no-one.
No-one shed tears for the cubs, the five-aside pitch or the bingo hall.
The merger of the primary schools happened, and no-one held a banner.
The hospital relocated and no-one soaked their skin in kerosene and threw their flaming corpse at the wheels of the departing ambulance.
When the mega-store put the main street out of business and then fucked off after a year, no-one commandeered a jumbo jet and eased it into a nose dive.

No-one did all that.

But so what?
Why should I care?
I've got problems of my own mate.
Look at me.
Here.
I fucking hate this place.
I'm out to get it.

But not everyone's like me.
Good folk affiliate.
Good folk intervene.
Know what I mean?

>:*I wish I could make someone really happy.*

Michael   You shouldnae be watching that.

Ty   How?

Michael   It's not your house.

Ty	It's not *your* house.
Michael	I'm not watching it. God look at this. (*Sings*) "Your lipstick marks still on my coffee cup…"
Ty	Say again.
Michael	I therefore deduce my dear Watson, that he hasn't done the dishes since his Gran left. And that was months ago. So. That's another thing. To add to the list. (*Sings*) "I've got a fist of pure emotion, I've got a face of shattered teeth…" Time?
Ty	Dunno. Maybe he's not coming.
Michael	He'll be here.
Ty	Yeah. I won't though man. I'm off.
Michael	What? How?
Ty	Michael. A guy has a problem you…kinda…punch him on the arm, buy him a pint and tell him that shit happens. This intervention stuff is for American women.
Michael	Ach it's no big deal. We're saying we're worried that's all. Shows we care. It's common practice.
Ty	Aye in America. This is New Flood. No-one cares about anything.
Michael	Not true Ty. Not true. If you'd come to the Common Good meetings, you'd know there's a small group of citizens who *do* care. Very much so. In fact……well. Can't say too much. Just…watch this space.
Ty	Whatever man. I'm going. I can't do it.

Michael	Who else is going to do it? His dad's dead, his mum's dead, his gran's run off. Who else? We're his best pals man. The Three Thingbys. Amigos. And if I'm honest, now hear me out, I think that Vincent might be closer to *you* than he is to me.
Ty	For God sake Michael…
Michael	Don't say another word. I know all about it.
Ty	Thank you! Of course you do.
Michael	Of course I do. You feel bad cos you've not been there for him since Arlene left. Well so do I. All the more reason to stay. And anyway you can't go. If there's two guys it's an intervention – if there's one guy it's just a nosy twat telling him to do his dishes. Please. Sit down. Watch the TV.
Ty	It's not my house.
Michael	Well look at these again.
Ty	I've seen them.
Michael	Not properly. You've got to really *look* cos of the blurring. I tell you, that's the last time I buy a camera from Lightning Rod.
Ty	Don't know why you still give the guy business. I've still got the burns from that fucking mobile he sold me.
Michael	Mobile phones are extremely prone to fires.
Ty	Only if you buy them from Lightning Rod. (*About the photos.*) Very nice.
Michael	He's beautiful eh?

Ty	Say again.
Michael	Beautiful. Do you think em…?
Ty	What?
Michael	Nah. Nothing. Do you think he looks like me?
Ty	Eh?
Michael	Does he look like me? To you. Or Pamela? At all.
Ty	Ooooooh ha ha ha! Doubting the parentage eh? Give us them back a minute I wasn't really looking.
Michael	Ha! No he's just too beautiful to be mine that's all. Ha ha h… you know

> Vincent
> Michael's got a breakdown of his own at home.

> Michael
> Pamela. For God sake I wasn't accusing you of anything. I just said the baby was perfect. Okay I said "too perfect" but that's a good thing. So what if he doesn't look like us yet. Kids don't look like anyone until they put a uniform on mark my words. And no-matter what your bloody mother says, the chances of babies getting switched in the

29

wards are slim. I just…I…I just don't see *us* in him. Do you? He has no imperfections. I haven't felt that connection. Yet. Yet. I wish I could make you happy. Really happy but…. ach, look, let's just put all this down to stress.

It's very stressful having kids. It's a horrible world if you think about it. It's not just Burger Kings. It's text speak and chat rooms and every where you look an idiot. It's very worrying.

Ty   Well I can put your mind to rest on one point.

Michael   What?

Ty   He's not mine.

Vincent   What this? An intervention?

Ty   How did you know it's an intervention?

Vincent   They're common practice.

Michael   Well! Hello hello. This isn't quite…I wanted to…

Vincent   What? Jump out in the dark? "Surprise! You're a fucking loser!"

Michael   No…

Ty	I've never heard of the bloody things.
Vincent	Well you're not exactly "up to date" are you?
Ty	Say again.
Vincent	How did you get in?
Ty	The back door's always open innit.
Michael	Vincent…
Vincent	Wine? It's blood warm and fizzes like piss. Any takers? Well if you insist.
Michael	Vincent. Listen, you've obviously been expecting this so…I mean you can't just hit the skids and get away with it. What about us? You're thirty years old man. Responsibilities, family, career, social life. All that horrible shit. You're throwing that all away mark my words. So. You know. We're worried. We care. There. Said it.
Vincent	Very nice.
Michael	So don't get angry.
Vincent	I'm not angry.
Michael	Inside you are. And this, this is all about…well…you know…
Vincent	What?
Michael	Love.
Vincent	Love.
Ty	Not love. He doesn't mean…more a kinda like…kinda like…you know what I mean.

Michael	Aye. Well. The important thing is that we all admit you're having a breakdown and take it from there.
Vincent	I'm not having a breakdown.
Michael	C'mon now, play the game. We've admitted it.
Vincent	But I'm not having a breakdown. Who said you could watch my TV by the way?
Ty	I'm not watching it.
Michael	Oh come on mate. Just admit it. You've been drunk every night for three months, pissing yourself in the street.
Vincent	Once.
Michael	You've been in fights, you stink, the house is a tip…
Vincent	I stink?
Michael	You've been phoning me up at the council, don't deny it, phoning me up drunk at the council and calling me a, for want of a better word, cunt. Vandalising monuments, sabotaging the Greetings From New Flood sign, leaving these mad letters all over town. Which, by the way, all have your name at the bottom. It all points to one thing. You son, are having a breakdown.
Vincent	I think you'll find those letters are art.
Michael	Art? Art is it? How are they art? If they were art they'd be in a gallery.
Vincent	You shut the gallery.
Michael	Funding.

Vincent	What do you think of the letters?
Ty	I dunno. Kinda. I dunno.
Vincent	The man on the street speaks. Here, he's aimless and unemployed, why isn't he getting an intervention?
Michael	Firstly, Ty's not wasting potential...
Ty	Say again.
Michael	And secondly, Ty didn't write this and leave it on every bench in New Flood.
Vincent	

Dear Mr Dylan,

Thank you for your letter dated July 14th. I must admit it caused a great deal of excitement in the office, it's not often we receive a Sales Invoice from a star of your grace and magnitude.

In answer to your question, I do not remember agreeing to a fixed price for all the tarpaulin used in the job.

However, I do remember one day at school our teacher took us to the beach. We all wrote a wish on a piece of paper, put it in a balloon and watched as they floated away. My wish was too heavy. My balloon burst.

I shall be released,

Vincent Watts.

Michael	If you put that amount of effort into finding a job you wouldn't be pissing yourself in public as much, mark my words.

Vincent	Well it's alright for you Michael, your wish was lighter than mine.
Michael	Eh? Look… I don't remember any of that. And I don't make wishes anymore and neither should you. We're adults and we're here to……
Vincent	What? Fix me?
Michael	No…
Vincent	How can I be fixed? Tell me what to do. Tell me.
Michael	Well. You could…
Vincent	What?
Michael	You could…
Vincent	What?
Ty	You could do your dishes.
Michael	Aye.
Doorbell	
Michael	That's probably for me.
Vincent	Eh?
Michael	(*As he exits to answer the door.*) And anyway, any forward step has to come from you. We don't have all the answers Vincent. I'd love to see you come up with a plan or an idea or something to show you were taking part in the world again. I'd back you 110% I really would. But it has to come from you.
Vincent	Who's this now? Another guest on This Is Your Fucked Up Life.

Ty   Dunno. Listen. He made me come. He thinks it's all
            about your Gran leaving or something…I…didn't…
            so…I couldn't…you know what I mean.

Vincent   Yeah yeah. So…

Ty   So.

Vincent   How are you anyway?

Ty   Dunno. Alright. You?

Vincent   What do you think, I'm in the middle of a fucking
            intervention.

Ty   Oh. Yeah.

Ty   Listen…

Michael   Unbelievable! Unbelievable! Sorry Vincent, I told
            Sweeny to find me as soon as he heard.

Sweeny   Good evening.

                              Vincent
                              Sweeny.
                              The softly spoken
                              chemist from the days
                              of wooden counters.
                              He shouldn't be here.

Ty   Looking very dapper Mr Sweeny.

Sweeny   Nice to be dapper. It's a wonderful day.

                      Vincent   Oh aye.

35

Michael	Listen folks we have to bolt. Emergency meeting of The Common Good Committee.
Sweeny	A wonderful, wonderful day.
Vincent	So to clarify. You break into my house, tell me I'm a failure, force me into having a breakdown and now you're going?
Sweeny	How did the intervention go may I ask?
Vincent	For f…
Michael	Personal stuff Mr Sweeny. I'll tell you in the car.
Ty	Can I get a lift?
Sweeny	Ah.
Michael	No time Ty. Vincent, we've done our bit, pointed out our concerns. The rest is up to you. Start with the dishes by all means, but make those changes.
Vincent	What fucking changes? Whoah! Wait a minute. What's going on?
Sweeny	We won.
Michael	Sssh now. I don't think we should…
Vincent	Won what?
Sweeny	Won the competition.
Michael	Sweeny…
Vincent	What competition? I swear to God Michael I'll fucking…
Michael	Okay, okay. Alright tell them.

Sweeny	New Flood, has been named today, as the Worst Town In Scotland. Officially. It is a wonderful day.
Michael	Yup. There it is. Out in the open. Great eh? Look, they're in shock. It's all down to us you know. The Common Good Committee. Me, Sweeny, Mrs Young. It's a dream come true. Look, they can't believe it.
Vincent	Oh no, I can *believe* it. Just...isn't this...a *bad* thing?
Sweeny	Oh no no no.
Michael	Oh no no no. It's a very, very good thing.
Vincent	Why?
Michael	Why? I'll tell you why. It's a very, very good thing Vincent old champion, because the Worst Town In Scotland, gets...
Vincent	Five Hundred Thousand Pounds. From a multi-national communications company who, for the sake of this story, would prefer to remain faceless. To work out who's THE WORST they use a formula stolen from the UN. It's called The Human Development Index. In this formula everything has a symbol; Life expectancy, literacy, income, employment, infant mortality and *you*. You have a symbol. These symbols are added, subtracted, divided and multiplied and in the end there's a LIST Canada to the top, Sierra Leone to the bottom.

But *this* set of awards is just for Britain.
It proves, to someone somewhere, that this evil
conglomerate *cares* about people and community, and
is more than willing to publicly dump its tax
deductible charity contributions on shitholes up and
down the country, in the hope that one day, we can
achieve our dream of equality:
All of us using the same top-end picture messaging
phone, on the same network.

So who wins?
Well, it turns out that Glasgow's Miles Worse;
They'll be dancing in the streets of Shettleston,
Springburn, and Parkhead as they get the bulk of the
Scottish dosh.

But Sweeny found a loophole

> Sweeny
> I found a loophole.

You see none of these places are *towns*.
And there's a special award for towns.

> Sweeny
> If you look closely.

And not many do.
And if you know the formula too

> Sweeny
> You can be creative
> with your symbols.

Of course it's a smaller amount of money.
In real terms, 500 grand will do very little,
But think of it...

Michael

> Think of a youth centre
> where kids can go and
> be protected from all
> the idiots in the world.
> Where they can stay
> perfect, away from the
> endless junk that's
> thrown at them these
> days. Think of the
> peace of mind.

Mrs Young

> Think of the public
> meetings. The
> community spirit. The
> hand shakes, kisses and
> royal visits. Think of all
> the friends together.
> Celebration.
> Celebration.

Sweeny

> Think of all the eyes at
> the champagne
> reception. Think of the
> flashbulbs and that
> perfect vindication.
> Think of where this
> could take us…

Michael   Let's go!

Sweeny   Cheerio.

Ty   I kinda better get going too. Know what I mean.

Vincent	Aye I know what you mean. So this is it mate. Bottom of the barrel. I am the Worst Person in the Worst Town in Scotland. Officially. "I'd love to see you come up with a plan or an idea or something to show you were taking part in the world again. I'd back you 110% I really would." Arsepiece. He's not an artist. He's never done anything important. I'd like to come up with a scheme alright, a scheme to bring this place to its fucking knees. Not just vandalism or prank calls. Something big. Then I'd just walk away, like you've all walked away from me.
Ty	How have we walked away? We're in your fucking house, trying to help.
Vincent	Help? He was gloating. And what were you all about eh? Sitting there like his fucking lap dog "can I get a lift?"
Ty	You know I think you love this, man. I'm right here you know.
Vincent	Well don't let me keep you.
Ty	You know what, I'd love to see you come up with a scheme to bring this place to its fucking knees. I'd back you 110% I really would. Cos I think what you do is art, or it used to be. But to make New Flood worse, that would be a kinda…masterpiece. And you could do with one of those.
Vincent	Aye on you go. Fuck off. I'm still an artist! There's a masterpiece on its way son. Watch this space.

> Tupelo Tam
>> Heroes are forever.
>> They're very important.
>> They help you get up in

the morning. So choose
your heroes with care.

Vincent   The first piece of art in my life wasn't a picture at all.
           It was a space I watched on a wall where a picture
           used to be. When mum was wee, back in the 60s,
           when the world was full of icons, only one image
           mattered in her house. Instead of fairy tales, she would
           sit under the portrait of Bob Dylan that covered their
           living room wall and listen to Tam wax lyrical......

Tam   What goes on behind those shades eh? Some kind of
           genius. He's the history of America; all the howls and
           glory, all its struggles wrapped up in the hippest of
           the young, the oldest of the voices. I hear the films of
           John Ford in that voice and the stories of Twain, I hear
           the passion of Dr King and the roar of the pop groups
           and all those also-rans that sound so puny beside him.
           He's politics and poetry. He's true, Grace. That's all
           you're looking for. Truth.

Grace   Mum says he takes drugs.

Tam   So what if he does? He's an artist. He uses them to
           expand his art. Nothing wrong with that is there?

Grace   No. I like the tambourine song.

Tam   You're a good girl.

                         Vincent
                         For Mum, Bob was
                         more than a hero. He
                         was like an ancient
                         God. So of *course* she
                         worshiped him as a
                         child. Like she
                         worshiped her dad. And
                         when she got thrown

left right and centre by
adolescence, of *course*
she grew to lust him.

Grace creeps into the living room and quietly removes the picture of Mr Dylan. She props it up and caresses it. She starts to masturbate. Tupelo Tam enters, casting a wedge of light from his opening door onto the horrible scene. They don't speak.

Vincent   For Tam it was all over. The picture was removed. He
            sank into his chair and stopped speaking in coherent
            sentences. And mum? Well, she wasn't a good girl
            anymore. She slipped into the habit of disappointment
            and all the shit that brings. All was defiled. All
            destroyed. Until...

Phone rings

Arlene   I'm getting that am I?

Tupelo   mmmmmmmmmmmm
ssssssssssssssssssssssssssssssssshhhhhhhhhhhhhhhhhhhhhhhhhhhhhhhhhhhhhhhhhhhhhhhhhhhhhhhhhhhhh

Arlene   Is it you? Oh God what is it hen? Are
            you...just...what is it? Grace doll I...don't know what
            to do..................

Vincent   Tupelo Tam is running
            Backwards in time.
            Back to make everything all right again with his
            daughter,
            And with his understanding, the song returned

                 >: Like a complete unknown...like a rolling
            stone.
            So for Tupelo Tam his hero returned with a burst of
            truth right in the heart

42

And I was born with the pull of the high rise inside
me.
The dread that took my mother, took Tupelo and
Gran,
Is in me already and sounding out.

ta toom   ta toom.

Michael
    Which is why we have
    to have an intervention.

Ty What's an intervention?

Michael
    They're common
    practice.

Ty Don't you think it
    would be…
    kinda…awkward me
    being there?

Michael
    How?

Ty Well.

Michael
    What?

Ty Oh come on. You *must*
    know. Everyone knows.

Michael
    What?

Ty Me and Vincent…

Michael
    Understand each other.
    I know. It's the art isn't
    it? I just cannae
get it.
    I mean, how can vandalising road signs
Be art?

Vincent   I take it you're unaware of the work of Tom Tom, François Morel or Heath Bunting?

Michael   I'm aware someone made a sign saying "Greetings From New Flood: It's Worse Than It Fucking Looks". I'm aware of that.

Vincent   It's called subvertising.

Michael   It's called…flipping…pish. It's done in council colours and stencilling Vincent, that's the thing. This is an inside job mark my words. Heads'll roll. I have a duty to blow this caper wide open. So. Who's your connection?

Vincent   My connection?

Michael   Don't give us it. You obviously have a friend that works in the council and you've used his or her name to procure paints and…aw shit you never! Well we can't mention this right? I mean ever.
    I tell you man this time
        He's gone too far. We
        have to step in.

      Ty Aye okay. But I'm not
          making a speech or
          anything.

      Michael
        No worries.

I'll just very camly say to him
Ho! Wanker. Aye you! Ya wanker. We don't like
wankers in this school so you'd...AAAH!

Ty punches Michael. Flattens the fucker.

Vincent
> I can't remember when
> Michael changed from
> the arsehole he was then
> into the arsehole he is
> now.
> But it's a fair bet that it too,
> started with a punch.

Ty   He called me a wanker.

Vincent I know he's a dick. He's not tough or anything. He
only does this with new folk and a wee guy called Rod
that got hit by lightning. Rod never fights back in
case God punishes him again.

Ty   Yeah. Well I fight back.

Michael That was total agony ya spazzy. No offence Vincent.
You're dead by the way. I'm fucking grassing.

Ty   Go on then ya fudd.

Michael Fucking will ya...

Ty   What?

Michael Ya... fucking...poof.

Vincent
> Although if you ask
> Michael, he first met
> Ty...

Michael
> When we were on the
> same football team in
> high school. It was
> mutual respect from the
> opening whistle.

Vincent
> For us, the opening
> whistle was a line
> crossed on a school trip
> to Butlins. Agony aunts
> say "experimentation"
> but it wasn't as
> controlled as that for
> Ty. It felt good that's
> all. So he did it. It came
> from the same place as
> the fist that smashed
> Michael's face. And
> that's the great thing
> about him. He's a force
> of nature. He lives on
> instinct. Me, I'm all
> narration. Everything I
> do is contrived and
> commented on in my
> head; "you're giving the
> impression of
> spontaneity. This is a
> good thing".

He wasn't like me in any way.
That was the attraction.
It was all new. I got to be a new person. Cos
No-one's ever felt like us.

Ty   Keep going.

Vincent   No love song's got us sussed.

Ty   Keep going.

Vincent   Cos we're the centre of the universe. When we're
           making love I feel like we're pulling all the planets,
           all the stars, suns and comets closer and closer in to
           us.

Ty   That's it.

Vincent   Even God stops what he's doing and watches us fuck…

Ty   Okay shut it now that's putting me off.

Vincent   Sounds cool though eh?

Ty   Yeah. Shut it.

Vincent   You don't care about the way I look, do you? Do
           you?

Ty   Vincent for fuck sake.

Vincent   Okay okay.   He didn't.   It wasn't that.
                                       It wasn't.
                                       It was the secrecy that
                                       wore us out. But it had
                                       to be a secret. There
                                       were no recorded cases
                                       of homosexuality in
                                       New Flood. There was
                                       a woman who looked a
                                       bit like a man and
                                       called herself Jim, but
                                       all she did was walk
                                       dogs. She was allowed.
                                       Our big bang would

> never be forgiven if it
> should ever come out.
> And of course, it did come out.
> On our last day at school.
> It just…it…it…

Ty   Just tell me or I swear I'll rip your face to fucking pieces.

Vincent   It wasn't me I promise. I love…Ah!

Ty   Someone wrote it.

Vincent   Not me. Ah!

Ty   This is what you want isn't it ya fucking…

Vincent   Don't!

Ty   It had to be you. Fuck man. Fuck. Everyone saw.

> Vincent
> Everyone saw. It was a
> virus in the school, an
> epidemic in the town.
> Everyone saw. It was as
> if the graffiti on the bog
> wall was written in foot
> high letters of blood.

VINCENT

loves

TY

IF DESTROYED TRUE
IF NOT DESTROYED TRUE

Arlene	I don't know what to do.
Vincent	It's not true.
Arlene	Cos if it is…
Vincent	It's not but.
Arlene	I wish I knew what to do. No-one teaches you. This is the time I should just be your Gran. A second chance at being a mother. But…I still don't know what to do. I've seen my baby jump and I've wanted to reach out from behind and grab you. Save you. But I don't know how.
Vincent	I'm not falling but.
Arlene	Do you know what I should do?
Vincent	No.

> But someone did.
>> Ty's dad was a soldier who'd come to New Flood to play golf and hide. He heard the gossip in a pub. He knew what to do. He kicked down doors till his son was screaming…

Ty   I *am* a man! I am! I am a *man*! Please. *I* fucking *am*. I *am*! I am a man! I am a man. I am. I'm…………………………………………

> Vincent
>> It was an ugly swing with a trusty five iron

49

that put the hole in Ty's
right ear drum.
No-one forgot. They
just stopped talking
about it. It was
ammunition now; in
case we should try
something, years down
the line. Like being big
shots or wise guys or
smart alecs, you know,
all those things that this
place hates. Then the
ammunition would
come out and we'd get
shot in the heart like
the dogs we were.

Still together though,
on and off. Lovers when
drunk, all through our
terrible twenties. But
the secret was dirty
now. The "love" part of
it was an
embarrassment in the
mornings after those
one night stands. It was
the love part that ruined
it. And then one day
it was gone.
And I'm amazed because
This self hatred/denial thing's like something from a
fucking museum.

Ty   I'm not in denial I know what I am.

Vincent   Do you?

Ty	What's that meant to mean?
Vincent	I mean it would be nice if you at least admitted…
Ty	This is me admitting it!
Vincent	Is it? I dropped out of art school for you. Us.
Ty	You were thrown out.
Vincent	Cos I was here all the time! Hoping you'd realise what century you were living in.
Ty	I never asked you to stay.
Vincent	Yes you did! You did! The night you got turned down by the army cos of your ear. You made me promise never to leave town.
Ty	I was upset.
Vincent	Upset? Oh your life's been a total tragedy. Boo hoo hoo.
Ty	It's finished. That's all. Finished.
Vincent	Heard it.
Ty	Well. I mean it now. It's just not *me*.
Vincent	It was you the other night at Michael's tapas thing. It was you in their spare room under the coats. That's the real you Ty. I'm just telling you, that's what you are.
Ty	You're not listening! I'm not denying I'm gay Vincent. I'm not scared of coming out, fuck, I *am* out. I'm not saying that. What I'm saying is… I need something else. Something apart from this.

Vincent   ....right.

Ty   So it's finished.

Vincent   It'll...I'll have nothing left Ty. Nothing. I'll be...

Ty   Look. It's amazing it lasted as long as it did. It could never work in a place like this anyway. It just couldn't.

        Vincent
        When I got home that night, three months ago, broken hearted and alone, I found a letter. The timing was exquisite. It was from Gran.

Arlene

Dear Vincent,

I'm away son. I've stood by you the best I could, but if I don't find out what I'm supposed to do I'll shrivel up and die.

I wish I could've caught you. All of you. But I didn't.   I need to learn how to do that. I know you won't miss me much, after a week or so.

However, I do remember a nice time. Eating crisps on a towel on the beach and Grace playing in the sand and your Granddad put his hand on my shoulder. I'm leaving because that's the nicest thing about them that I can remember.

Bad things have happened to us, we've been crushed, I know. But it's up to us to change our lives and to make what wishes are left come true.

When I come back I'll catch you. I promise.

I shall be released,

Arlene.

Vincent

And that's the way it
always is. Just when
you think everything's
destroyed something
comes along and makes
it worse. That's art
man. Art's a
destructive thing. For
me anyway. It's a
problem causer. It's a
gap on a wall and a
letter on the
mantelpiece. It's an
abusive road sign and a
limp. It's a reason for
splitting up. Ty's right.
I should practise what I
preach and make it
worse.
Aye. Make it worse.
"That would be a kinda
masterpiece."

Michael   It would be the youth centre to end all youth centres,
right here in New Flood! A place that's safe. A place
that educates. Properly educates, like the old days;
you know with jotters and sums and facts that folk
remember. Where we can force them to read books
and play sports and hate stuff that's rubbish. A place
that takes them off the streets away from their mobiles
and laptops and Chicken Royales.

Mrs Young	Doesn't the school do that kind of thing?
Michael	School? School is it? School? I assume you know that the schools are in chaos Mrs Young. Know what they found in a sink the other day in the Academy? A toley. A toley. In a sink. I mean come on. I tell you, the world is a terrifying idiot.
Mrs Young	Really?
Michael	Mark my words. And this place wouldn't be like school. It would be fun and trendy and would involve words like, "dude" and "wicked".
Mrs Young	"Groovy". Is that a word?
Michael	Well it's a word…
Sweeny	Something like the BBs, as was?
Michael	Aye. Only less sinister. And everyone would benefit, not just the kids. There'd be a venue the whole town could use and we'd be churning out perfect wee citizens, one by one. And there'd be jobs. And crime would go down.
Mrs Young	Oh crime. Did I tell you that three nights ago someone broke my aerial clean off? Yes. A young lad. I shouted at him and he came right up to me, right onto my step, holding the aerial like a, like a…
Michael	Lightsaber.
Mrs Young	Bread knife. And he said some…horrible things. He painted quite a picture. I haven't slept straight through since. He lives right across the road too. Number 15. He's called Norman. To him I must look like a silly old woman with no friends. I suppose that must have something to do with it.

Michael	This is what I'm talking about. Under my scheme wee Norman would've spent his day rooting through rock pools and fixing inner tubes and all that guff. By night-time his cheeks would be too ruddy for breaking aerials.
Mrs Young	Yes. Well it's definitely something to bring up at the public meeting.
Michael	Public meeting! What's it got to do with the public? We did this. We're the ones who show up to the Common Good Committee every second Wednesday not them. It should be us that decides. They've never shown the slightest interest in doing something that we can all share in. Selfish swine. But bet you anything this place is packed when they hear there's 500 grand on the go…
Sweeny	And photos needing taken.
Michael	And giant cheques to hold up. It'll be like Glastonbury in here mark my words.
Sweeny	Well, I have taken the liberty to make us signatories on the account. All of our names are required to release any funds so *we're* here for keeps, no matter what the swine are planning.
Michael	Good man.
Sweeny	But I'm rather ashamed to say there's been a bit of a silly mix up. You see they've put me down as Chairman, Michael as Treasurer and Mrs Young as Secretary. I don't know how…
Michael	Well that's alright. Who cares? I assume you don't mind if Sweeny's the new Chairman do you Mrs Young?

Mrs Young	Well…
Michael	Of course not. What's in a title? Less of a burden for you Mrs Young.
Mrs Young	Well…
Sweeny	Which leads me on…I'm afraid to say that the Youth Centre idea seems a bit far fetched for the funds available Michael. Perhaps if it were £750,000 or a million then yes, it would be…
Michael	But it's a start though isn't it? We'd buy a place, do it up and when it all turns to crap, shame the council into finishing the job. It's common practice. I've got connections.
Sweeny	Still…
Michael	And…
Sweeny	And I *am* the chairman and as such believe that we should perhaps move on.
Michael	Oh. Oh right. Well. (*To Mrs Young.*) It wasn't like this in your day.
Sweeny	I assume Mrs Young agrees with me.
Vincent	People have always assumed Mrs Young. They assume cats. They assume an ailing mother with errands. They assume the tea rooms of the National Trust. They assume a husband, dead or alive, and a busy life somewhere else. But she has none of these things.

Mrs Young
I can't imagine how it
feels to be kissed.
Sometimes I hold an
apple to my lips.

Vincent   She has given up replacing Mrs with Miss.

Mrs Young
Dear Lord, all I want is
to have a friend to visit
and drink tea with. I
crave it. Almost as
much as the baby days,
you remember those. I
haven't been in
someone's house now
for a year and three
days, as you know. No-
one invites me. No-one
asks if I ever get lonely
or if I'd like to join
them for tea next
Sunday. And I try to be
nice and smiley and
happy but…somehow
that moves them further
away.

Michael
So what do you say?

Mrs Young
He's beautiful.

Michael
> Aye but do you think
> he looks like me?
> Or…Pamela even?

Mrs Young
> I've never met Pamela.

Michael
> You should see the baby
> though. He really is
> perfect.

Mrs Young
> Oh I'd love to. I'd love
> to. I'd really *really* love
> to…

Michael
> You can't tell cos of the
> blurring but he is
> controversially perfect.
> Oh well. We all have
> our troubles. See you at
> next week's meeting
> then.

Mrs Young
> Oh. Right.

Vincent   She lived her life from the centre of plastic tables
pulled together.
And here she has her highs and lows.
On committees when no-one else would go, she was
present, busy, smiling on.
And now in a stroke, her role, right in the centre of
her own wee world was destroyed.

She was no longer chairperson, and "her day" was gone.

Mrs Young   I have something to say……

Michael   Vincent! What the hell are you doing here?

Sweeny   Perhaps the intervention didn't take?

Michael   Listen mate we're in a meeting, can this wait?

Vincent   It's about the money. The Worst Town in Scotland money. That's what you're talking about right? Well, I've got an idea.

Michael   It's a bit late in the day to express an interest in joining the committee Vincent. (*To Sweeny.*) See what I mean?

Vincent   Of course I'm not expressing an interest in joining the committee. I've just got an idea about spending the money that's all. But it's, well it's…it's a bit…dodgy.

Michael   What do you mean, dodgy?

Sweeny   Illegal.

Vincent   Not quite. Right, I was thinking, 500 grand isn't that much is it? It won't go far, not if you're trying to make the whole town a better place? And I take it that's the point. You get the cash and have to spend it on something that will make New Flood a better place right?

Michael   Of course.

Vincent   And is there any rule that says you can't win the award two years in a row?

Sweeny	No no no. In fact parts of Glasgow have been receiving the award for a decade, but their problems are far more widespread and…
Vincent	Okay okay. Well my idea right, is to put half the cash in the bank and let it gather some heavy interest. Meanwhile you spend the remaining 250, not on making the town *better*, but on making it *worse*. So that way, we win again next year and maybe even the following year. By always saving some of the money as you go along, you'll soon have enough cash to do something that really makes a difference. Something that will actually change New Flood for the better. Not just a token gesture. Of course it would have to *look* like you were trying to do good, while all the time you were doing bad, and it'll have to be *really* bad to keep the town at the bottom of the list. Which is, of course, the dodgy bit. But I'm sure one of you clever folk could figure something out. So. What do you think?

TA TOOM   TA TOOM   TA TOOM

Vincent	Mrs Young was thinking

> Mrs Young
> A ball is rolling and it's
> going to crush me. Or
> just ignore me and how

Vincent	Mr Sweeny looks taller

TA TOOM   TA TOOM

Vincent	He's thinking of his sudden erection and a perfect recollection of

Sweeny

> One of the swine,
> shamelessly naked.
> Indecent in her
> condition. I'm teaching
> her a hard lesson.
> People like her
> shouldn't be allowed to
> breed. Who is she to
> tell me about being
> good? I have cooked
> her many a
> "prescription" over the
> years, and even if she
> couldn't pay, we would
> find a way to feed her
> repulsive addiction.
> And yet she still tries to
> trick me. Some people
> will never learn. And
> should fade away, for
> the common good.
> That's the thinking…

TA TOOM
TA TOOM
TA TOOM

Vincent   Of a man who to my mother was

Grace

> The Devil. If it's really
> his, then neither of us
> deserve to live. Either
> that or we deserve each
> other. What have I
> become? I want to run

away. But I can't. I
need to see what he has
in his bag. I need it.
Like family

Vincent   Who were in a wee house ten minutes away.   Where
Tam, who only ever thinks

Tam
I blame you for this.

Vincent   Knows he's wrong but won't admit it. Yet. Yet the
phone will ring and be answered by Arlene
sssssssssssssssssssssssssssssssssssssssssssssssssssssssssssssshhhhhhhhhhhhhhhhhhhhhhhhhhhhhhh

who is in Berlin, right at this minute, thinking that

Arlene
Youth Hostels are
lonelier than bus
stations and that's
saying something. This
will seem adventurous
when I get home.
They'll be amazed. I'll
just lie about the white
water rafting and
bungee jumping. That's
the stuff that proves
you've lived. Isn't it?
What if I never find the
answer? What if I still
don't know what to do?
Maybe no-one needs to
know. I wonder if
Vincent knows I'm
happy for him and Ty

toomttoomttoomttoomttoomttoomttoomttoomttoomttoomttoomttoomttoomttoomtoomtooomttoomttoo

Vincent   Who is wearing his father's old uniform. Something
           he does more and more

                              Ty Now he's gone. You can
                                  be anything you want
                                  underneath a uniform.
                                  People will always see it
                                  before they see the man.
                                  That's the power it has.
                                  I don't want power
                                  though. I want
                                  something else. To be
                                  tested, in a war
                                  or…something. Power
                                  on its own is for men
                                  like Michael

TOOMTTOOMTTOOMTTOOMTTOOM

Vincent   Whose mind is racing.

                              Michael
                                  There's the youth centre
                                  and all the good stuff
                                  that would bring. But
                                  are we really going with
                                  Vincent's thing? But
                                  for me or for him? Or
                                  for them? For reason or
                                  for fun? Or so I can
                                  run home and open that
                                  door and hold her in
                                  my arms. Happy again.
                                  A success at something.
                                  A man. For her.

toom   ta toom   ta toom   ta toom   ta toom

Vincent   And me I'm thinking about mum.
           As I sit on my bench.
           My masterpiece begun.
           Surrounded on all sides by the town
           And a sound
           That's neither a heartbeat nor a drum.
           I'm wondering what the hell could make this place
           worse.
           And what I'm going to do.
           And a phrase from somewhere years ago
           So and so loves so and so
           If destroyed true………

bee   bee
    boo   boo
           ccccck   ch

             cccccccccccccccccccccccccchhhhhhhhhhhhhhhhhhhh
                       ch   ch

           eeeeeeeeeeeeeeeee
      cc   oo   oo
cc   oooooooooo   ooooo   kct
   eooo
   kh
  cchhh
 cccc
KKkc

>:*connected to remote computer*

Vincent   Let me introduce you to Norman.
               Remember Norman?
               Mrs Young's neighbour.
               The aerial abuser.
               Well he's the last guest to arrive at this party
               And like everyone else here, he has a secret.

>:*verifying user name and password*

Vincent   Norman's modem clears its throat with a wheeze and a
               whistle
               Like an angry little Scottish animal.
               His heart skips, as it always does.
               And he's in.
               Straight to their chatroom rendezvous.
               Like a lot of the worst things in life
               It was once funny.

A crowd of Norman's mates, logging on to the New
Flood chat-room with women's names,
Having a virtual laugh at lonely folk.
Norman's fake name was Lucille.

Norman Yous ur total dafties by the way. No way man check it
oot. Some cunt cawed Zippy's talking tae us noo.

>:*Hi Zippy. My name's Lucille. An I've been
gagging to meet a zany fudd called Zippy. So I huv.*

He's lat, me and you huv a connection Lucille.
L. O. L. Fuck's at?

>:*Eh?*

Aw. Laughs out loud. Dobber.

>:*Here Zippy. Dae yi want tae sniff my scants?*

Heh heh heh. Lucille's a total heavy hoor.

Vincent But she wasn't really.
Norman's pals soon went home, but he stayed on line.
Only this time it wasn't so funny.
And Lucille talked till 4 am.
And she appeared again the very next night, leaning
on the chat room wall, running her fingers through
her thick black hair and laughing out loud.
And it made Norman feel great.
And night after night as his family stared at sitcoms
downstairs,
Lucille danced and sang and brushed the cheeks of
men she'd never meet,
In a steady blue light.
Night after night.

Norman Ha! No way man.

> *>:That's sooooo u. When r u guys going 2*
> *confront yr abandonment BS and * wise up*? [LOL].*

Vincent   Despite the impression she made on her first visit to
the chatroom, Lucille was an old fashioned woman.
She had Hollywood class and an enigma
That caused terrified men to seek her
And made what happened all the worse.

Norman   What the fuck's going on? Fuck! Someone......some
cunt's got Lucille.

> Vincent
> Norman had lost
> control,
> Someone out *there* was
> in his computer.
> Using Lucille.
> Describing her doing
> things she would never
> do.
> Pulling her into a dark
> corridor of the
> chatroom where no-one
> goes.
> Dragging her by the
> hair, folding her
> clothes. And they'd
> blocked Norman out.
> He was powerless.
> Forced to read the
> descriptions of Lucille's
> degradation.

> *>: LUCILLE: No, u r hurting me. [BLEEDS.*
> *TURNED ONTO HER STOMACH. LEGS KICKED*
> *WIDE]*

>: *ZIPPY:. I'm going to teach you a hard lesson.*
[LOL. PUTS HIS

Norman   Naw! Naw! Fucking…help!

                              Vincent
                                    Norman's fingers too
                                    sweaty, too shaky to fix
                                    this.
                                    It's called virtual rape.
                                    And it's common
                                    practice.

Norman   Help. Someone. I cannae…

          >: *ZIPPY: Shut up. [PUTS A BAG OVER*
HER HEAD. REMOVES A

Norman   Whit…a bread knife? No. No wi a bread knife. No.
          Oh you *CUNT.* Oh! Fuck.

          >: *LUCILLE: [dies.]*

                              Vincent
                                    Lucille dies with all the
                                    horror in Norman's
                                    imagination.
                                    A horror that flung
                                    him from his monitor
                                    to the street
                                    Raging for Zippy's
                                    blood.

Norman   REVENGE! REVENGE!

                              Vincent
                                    It was the night of
                                    broken aerials.

Mrs Young	Hey you! You there. That's my car. I know who you are. Hey you that's my aerial.
Norman	Eh? Eh? You know me? Are you fucking Zippy? Is that it? Are you Zippy?
Mrs Young	I...I beg your pardon?
Norman	I'm fucking...I'm goanna take this fucking bread knife and fucking......
Vincent	So when Sweeny came a knocking Looking for Norman He was ready.

> Sweeny
> Norman, I have a
> proposition for you.

> Norman
> I'm all fucking ears.

>:I wish I could make someone really happy.

Vincent	I tell you man I feel great. I'm off the booze, I haven't been up to the bench in days and, you'll be glad to know, the dishes are done. And all because of the plan. Making the worst town worse. Only in New Flood eh? The Stupidest Place In Britain. Officially.
Michael	Mmm. And you don't think there's any... moral problems?
Vincent	Don't give us it, when you worked out how much cash the town would get in five years your eyes lit up with

lemons. Ding ding ding! Anyway, it's art. Morals don't come into it. All art is revenge.

Michael   My eyes lit up cos I really want to do something good for the town Vincent. I know you're on some self-destruction kick, but this might actually help folk. In the long run. I hope. Sweeny's making a speech in a few days, telling the town the plan. I'm shitting it.

Vincent   How? What is the plan? I cannae wait man.

Michael   Oh it's…em…it's a humdinger. Mark my words. But secret. Watch this space.

Vincent   I'll need to think about how I announce it..

Michael   Announce what?

Vincent   What else? That it's a masterpiece of conceptual art.

Michael   Fuck that. This stays right under wraps. It's a five year plan man. It's only you that thinks it's an "art project" or whatever. To us it's politics. But if the public ever find out, it's misappropriation. It's a swindle. It's over.

Vincent   This is my chance though. I'll be known for this.

Michael   No. Sorry mate, but it'll ruin the whole thing. I can't risk that.

Ty   What whole thing? The back door was open again and I…

Ty is wearing his dad's uniform. Vincent and Michael laugh.

Ty   What? I don't see anything funny.

Michael   Try using your eagle eyes.

Ty   Say again.

Vincent & Michael
              "Love lifts us up where we belong…"

Ty   Ha ha. I've got a new job. They told me I had to
              provide my own uniform and this was all I had. What
              whole thing? What were you on about? Me?

Michael   No. Pamela. Talking of which, I'd better bolt. I want
              to hear the whole story behind this (*The uniform*.) in
              detail at a later date.

Vincent   Michael…

Michael   Sorry mate. Bigger fish. So hush hush.

Vincent   Prick. I dread to ask but…

Ty   Security guard. Kinda…heavy duty but. No laughing
              matter. I'm…this is it you know. Serious shit.

Vincent   What you guarding?

Ty   Monuments.

Vincent   Monuments?

Ty   They're under threat.

Vincent   Monuments are under threat? Who from?

Ty   Almost everyone. I'm the front line of the re-
              development scheme.

Vincent   Michael's scheme?

Ty	Sweeny's scheme. You know, the scheme to spend all that money. Help the town. A job for life. So. What do you think?
Vincent	I think…you shouldn't get too excited.
Ty	Right. Typical. You know I came straight here. Thought you'd be happy. I was going to apologise for the intervention and everything.
Vincent	No need, it worked.
Ty	So I see. I was going to ask you out for a pint. Celebrate the job, but you're not interested in anyone else apart from yourself are you?
Vincent	No I am, just that the job's a…
Ty	What? The job's a what?
Vincent	Nothing.
Ty	It's perfect Vincent. Perfect for me. I need something like this to kinda…balance shit out. Know what I mean. I'm gonna show folk what I'm made of. It could kinda change things.
Vincent	You're right. It is perfect. I'll come for that pint. Pint of Coke.
Ty	You can fill me in on Michael and Pamela. It's a shame innit?
Vincent	What?
Ty	Well she's put a lock on the bedroom door and having blood tests done on the baby. Wasn't that what you were talking about?

Vincent	Oh aye. Yeah it's a shame. What the fuck are the blood tests for?
Ty	To see who its parents are.
Vincent	Doesn't she know?
Ty	It's blurred.
Vincent	Michael told you that?
Ty	Lightning Rod.
Vincent	Ach that means nothing. He fucks everything up. They won't split up. They've been together since school.
Ty	That's it though. They see each other in the same way they always have. Sometimes you need to see folk in a different light eh? See them move on, or succeed, to remind you what it was you liked about them in the first place. Like, that they're still tough, or still impulsive and fiery…
Vincent	Or still artistic. Still visionary.
Ty	Yeah.
Vincent	Poor Michael. Locked out eh? Maybe we should have an intervention?

>: I wish I could make someone really happy.

Michael	Let me in. Look come on this is ridiculous. Mark my words. Let me in I have every right to be in there.
Norman	No-one gets in here. Committee meeting in progress.
Michael	Listen you, I *am* the committee.

Norman	You're history.
Michael	Who *are* you?
Norman	I'm Mr Sweeny's private army.
Sweeny	He means private secretary. Secretary I told you. Tsk. He's being trained up. Sorry Michael, come in, come in.
Michael	New desk I see? Chair?
Sweeny	Oh well. Nice to be dapper. Gives the people a feeling that we know what we're doing.
Michael	What *are* we doing? Who's that wee fanny?
Sweeny	A representation of youth. Possibly even of disillusioned youth. Either is good. Fresh perspectives on old problems. And he's a whiz at the electric computer.
Michael	I tried you at the shop but you're……
Sweeny	Concentrating my efforts on the town situation. It's a massive responsibility but I accept it humbly.
Michael	And Mrs Young is……
Sweeny	Sadly no more. In a Common Good sense. She feels her work has been done in winning the award and retirement inevitable. But I assume her mother is ill again, because the curtains stay closed. She has been good enough to put her name to a few cheques though so we've been moving forward steadily.
Michael	But we haven't had a meeting in weeks.

Sweeny	We're meeting now Michael. Oh don't feel left out. I make sure that your name is used at every opportunity. And in a sense, by doing this, are we not making your own plan a reality. The Youth Centre? You should be very proud.
Michael	Yeah. I have some ideas by the way. For making it worse.
Sweeny	Fabulous. I look forward to hearing them at some point in the future.
Michael	Well. Can't you hear them now?
Sweeny	Can I...? Hang on. Am I free to listen to Plan Pitches For The Backward Step Movement?
Norman	Naw.
Sweeny	My hands are tied you see. Bureaucracy at its most terrifying.
Michael	It's...just...
Sweeny	I tell you what. I will listen. Damn the red tape. He can do his worst. You can do your worst! Proceed.
Michael	Em...ahem...just...top of my head stuff. Compulsory Lottery Tickets. An Extravagant Bid To Host The Earth Summit. A Sexually Explicit Carnival, With Stabbings. A Slightly Downhill Ice Rink. A...
Sweeny	What are your genuine suggestions Michael?
Michael	Those...oh my genuine suggestions. Em...unemployment?
Sweeny	Unemployment.

Michael	Increase unemployment.
Sweeny	Right. How would we do that do you think? You could resign. But seriously son, we have the worst unemployment of any town in Scotland. I think you'll find that was one of the reasons we won the award in the first place. And that is our problem. All the traditional social ills are iller here than anywhere else: unemployment, health, income, education, crime. We're as low as we can go in those departments. And remember, all attempts must resemble a *forward* step. No, our attack has to be on a more sublime level. The level of humanity itself.
Norman	Humanity itself!
Sweeny	Nothing economical or social. That ball is already rolling. But spiritual…
Norman	Spiritual!
Sweeny	Psychological…
Norman	Psychological!
Sweeny	Personal…
Norman	Yes!
Sweeny	These levels are prime for attack. The human elements. What's human you may ask? Soul, purpose, depth…
Norman	Dignity, tradition, casual sex…
Sweeny	Ritual, individualism, permanence, meaning…
Norman	You name it.

Sweeny	The time is right boy. Most people are strangers to their own humanity.
Norman	Adrift from morality.
Sweeny	And it's our hope that it won't take much to…
Norman	Dis-Conn-Ect them.
Sweeny	Precisely. This is a taken-for-granted world Michael. You said as much yourself. A world of swine who don't mix with each other, know nothing of the arts or history and have fattened their bellies and minds with an excess of liberty. Too much of a good thing has allowed the Great Western Monster to slip loose its chains and trample its master. This is why our town is in ruins. You said as much yourself.
Michael	So. What is the plan?
Sweeny	The plan Michael, is to give them what they want.
Michael	Which is…?
Norman	Everything!
Sweeny	And nothing. Now is the time for empty rhetoric. Instead of wisdom they want information; instead of participation, access; instead of conversation, one way messaging; instead of authenticity, replication. They don't want to be people anymore, they want to be users, so we'll plug them in and let them use to their hearts' content. We give them all of those things. And New Flood will worsen. Mark my words.
Michael	What…computers or something?
Sweeny	There will, of course, be other factors to loosen them up. A bit of fear here and there oils the engine. So

don't mind the ugly rumours and security guards, they're here to keep the town *aroused*, that's all. The big idea is, as you so charmingly put it, computers or something. You see Michael any fool can accuse the clergy…

Norman   Harass the teachers…

Sweeny   Arm the police…

Norman   Fuck the nurses.

Sweeny   But what we're doing is sublime. We're teaching a hard lesson here. And we will be remembered for this.

                     Vincent
                        Sweeny's hatred made
                        him strong, he knew
                        that.
                        Just as he knew they
                        laughed behind his back
                        at University.
                        The struggling student,
                        stuck doing chemistry.
                        Dealing his drugs at
                        knock down prices just
                        to fit in with the cool
                        kids.
                        That's what they
                        thought.

Sweeny   Of course they were wrong.
              Why would I want to be one of the throng?
              They were the criminals, their morals gone.
              But later on they would come,
              In the middle of the night, begging me.
              Literally begging on their hands and knees.

Only then, when they were ruined and poor and infected would they see
That the cool calm centre of their universe was me all along.
And that's the way it has to be Grace.
It's a hard lesson I'm teaching here.
And some people never learn.
Although how I'd love it if you were to announce that you'd seen the error of your ways.
That you've seen in me an example,
And that from this moment on, live the dapper life.
That's my master passion.
So. Have you made the right decision?
Or do you want to see what I have in my bag?

Grace   I got the results through. So. It's definitely…yours.

Sweeny Ah.

Grace   You could be a good man. Clear my debts…

Sweeny I will not take morality from someone like you.

Grace   I could…we could be good. Somewhere else.

Sweeny Have I not been good? Is this not all about being good? Have I not been more of a father to you than Tupelo ever was. He ignores your pleas for help. He never visits with presents and caresses. He will never come running when you phone, delirious and begging. And yet you still try to…trick me. Lying to me. Like a child. Trying to discredit me. Well. I think we all know who's good and who's bad. So. Let me ask you again. Do you want to see what I have in my bag?

> Norman
> > I want to see what's in your bag.

79

Grace   I can't.

Sweeny   I tell you what. Let's forget this nonsense about test
             results. I have something…very special in here
             Grace. I've been keeping it just for you. For the
             common good. It's free. And you can have as much
             as you want.

                                 Norman
                                     Where did they come
                                     from?

                                 Sweeny
                                     The Balkans.

                                 Norman
                                     How come guns are
                                     always wrapped in
                                     chamois leather? You
                                     never see guns in, like,
                                     a gun box or something
                                     eh?

                                 Sweeny
                                     Just make sure they get
                                     fed into the eco system.

                                 Norman
                                     Eh?

                                 Sweeny
                                     I want to hear a big
                                     loud

Norman   Bang! Whi dae ye hink?

Ty   Is it real?

Norman   It widnae be wrapped in chamois leather if it wisnae
                real.

Ty   Where did it come from?

Norman   The Vulcans.

Ty   Say again.

Norman   So can ye handle this or whit?

Ty   I can handle it.

Norman   This is heavy duty. No laughing matter. Serious shit.
                It'll take a real man to dae this job properly.

Ty   I'll do it. I'll take the job. Can I ask you something?

Norman   Mr Sweeny has said all that needs to be said about the
                threat to these monuments, an what that does tae town
                pride. And what we have tae dae tae the swine that're
                laughing in oor faces with their graffiti! Laughing, as
                they take a fucking bread knife to oor fucking
                heritage an at! Who's a man noo, Zippy ya cunt, eh?
                Naw! Didnae fucking think so! That's what ye say.

Ty   Yeah…just point it though eh?

Norman   It's a hard lesson we're teaching here.

Ty   Right. No I was just going to ask…is it okay if I wear
                my own uniform?

Bee   bee
     boo   boo

                    cccccccccccccccccccccccccccccchhhhhhhhhhhhhhhhhhhhhhhhhhhhhhh

Sweeny	Ladies and gentlemen,
	As a member of the community of New Flood and the chairman of the Common Good Committee I, like you, have often asked, "why are we being punished for the failures of the past?".
	Isn't it time to create a history of the Now?
	Well, with the award of this money, we finally have a chance to be re-born.
	To achieve the Christian ideal
	And leave this wretched physical world behind.
	I say, let's EVOLVE.

From this day on, every household, business, institution in the town will be fitted, free of charge, with a high powered modem and internet connection. Those without the hardware will rent from us, the very latest systems. From this day on, our town will no longer be a struggling rural community, Looked down on by Them. But a thriving, connected, *online* community, envied by all.

From this day on, We will be Network Flood!

>:GREETINGS FROM NETWORK FLOOD...........

Think of it. No need to dread the hassle of the face to face, Of people adding their problems to yours. Or rue the days and hours you waste with thankless, physically demanding chores When all shopping, all banking, and everything that forces you out of doors Can, will and **must** be done online. In a fraction of the time.

Struggling businesses will seize the opportunity to
trade for themselves in the global community.
You are due a share of the profit being made on the
biggest high street imaginable, day after day.

Parents!
Why expel your precious ones to the wilds of over
crowded schools?
Why deliver them to incompetent teachers with
meagre resources,
When you can opt to have them educated one on one?
Them and the screen.
The biggest library the world has ever seen, is there at
the push of a button.
Ask your child, would they rather carry dusty books
and crumbling paper?
They'll tell you, downloaded digital video's better.

The unemployed can job-search the planet, but will
work from home.
The lonely will have lovers in Rio and Rome.
The darts league will beat teams from Las Vegas
The pubs will be chatrooms, but our anti-social days
are behind us.
Because we won't be social at all,
Or anything that They would call society.
Instead we'll have utopia,
Our town
Succeeding
Virtually.

Vincent
It is fucking genius!

Michael
Is it?

Vincent

> You're getting us to
> *voluntarily* shut the
> schools, close all the
> shops and whenever we
> want to do something
> social, lock ourselves
> alone in a room.
> You're taking away the
> only thing we had
> going for us: that we're
> all stuck here
> geographically,
> physically, a
> community cos we *have*
> to be.
> But not only do we
> tolerate the plan, we
> *want* it, cos it feels
> modern and cool and
> everyone gets a fucking
> computer to play with.
> Genius.

Michael

> I dunno. It's just the
> internet.

Vincent

> That's what everyone
> thinks, but it's not.
> You're replacing
> infrastructure, removing
> activity, forcing us to
> stop interacting.
> Forcing us. And they'll
> be no going back.

You're not an artist, you
don't see the big
picture. I do. It's
catastrophic. You're
going to make every
last one of us lonely.

Michael

I thought we were
already.

Vincent

When's the big switch
on?

Michael

Dunno. As soon as they
get hold of all the
equipment I suppose.
The whole town's
signed on for it. Could
be weeks.

Vincent

You're still on the
committee though eh?

Michael

Oh…aye. Still…you
know…pulling the
strings. Oh aye.

Vincent

Well maybe when
Pamela sees you're
finally doing something
important, things'll
change.

Michael
    Maybe.

Vincent
    You gonna be alright on
    the couch here?

Michael
    Oh aye, fine thanks.
    Cheers Vincent.
    Vincent?
    I've never made her
    happy.
    I tried, but…
    She's always thought
    there's something
    better, somewhere else,
    you know?
    But is that true?
    Maybe we should just
    be happy with what
    we've got.

Vincent
    What if what you've
    got's shite?

Michael
    That's what she said.
    We got the results back.
    From the hospital. He's
    ours.

Vincent
    Well. That's good.

Michael
    Yeah.

Vincent	It makes sense,
	When you're about to invest,
	To increase security.
	So here are cameras on the every street corner,
	The rising paranoia, the broken glass cemented under shiny barb wire.
	Here are the private guards on monuments, policing the beauty spots.
	Oiling the engine.
Ty	Who's there?
	I can see you.
	Fuckers.
	Just try it.
	This is serious shit.
	Who's a man now? Eh?
	Me.
	I am a man.
	Oh yes I fucking am. I am.

Being in love doesn't stop you being a man.
I'll tell him. Now I've got this, the job, the uniform, I can kinda see things clearer.
I am in love. *And* a man.
A man does this kinda thing.

Sturdy Oak.
Romantic when drunk.
Can't shop,
Can't talk to kids, can't control libido, can't talk to father.
Drink lager.
Love maps, keys, cars and gizmos.
Love current affairs, sport and war,
Value success, invent stuff,
Gets results.
Believe emotions complicate,

Masturbate.
I am a man. I'll tell him. Tomorrow. I'll say "Vincent.
My mistake. I still love…"

Who's there?
Eh?
Shit.
There's a kinda guard here.
There's an armed guard here.
You're not allowed up here…
Oh it's you.
What're you…?
Oh. Is it a test? Have I to…?
Fuck you doing?
No.

Ty struggles to get the gun from his holster.

Norman's gun goes off.
And blows a hole through Ty's gut.

He sees that his hands are covered in blood.
He sees that he's slumped against the monument.
Now is the time for vandalism

if

destr————————oyed

true

Sweeny

    I saw him on the
    computer in the
    library.
    That's his password.
    Zippy is such a strange
    name, it catches the eye
    you know.   Of course it
    might just be sheer
    coincidence but you
    know what these army
    types are like.
    Broom handles, bread
    knifes…

Norman

    I cannae mind telling
    you aboot aw this.

Sweeny

    Well, trauma plays
    funny tricks on the
    memory. I'm sure
    you'll do what's best for
    the common good.

>:TY:[dies.]

Norman   Who's a man noo…eh? Ya…who's a…who…

                                Sweeny

Vincent   Rocked by tragedy!
Climbs   Horrific gun crime.
To   Community stunned.
The   Pledges of vigilance
Roof   Zero tolerance.
                                     Vow to track down

Of
The
High Rise

Looking
Down
On
The
Bench,
The
Town.
Throwing
Away
Letters

perpetrator. All support
to visiting police and
camera crews.
Don't rule out drug
gangs, gay bashers or
race hate. Don't feel
safe.
The killer is out There.
All religions unite to
pray for brutal
vengeance. Children
should be protected and
 given gruesome details.
But we shall rise again.
Congregate as a town,
next week,
With the world
watching, as we switch
on the Network.
A symbol of hope in a
time of great darkness.
It's what Ty would have
wanted.

Vincent is ready

To fly.

He stretches out his arms,

He moves to the ledge.

The same position Grace took, before she fell.

And we are all of us

Falling.

So

Time to go.

> *>:I wish I could make someone really happy*

Vincent   (If not destroyed true)

But he can't

Take that last step

Not just because he's had second thoughts.

But because something is holding him back.

No.

Some<u>one</u> is holding him back

Arlene   You see.
              I caught you.

Vincent   Gran. Gran.

Michael   And I used to hate him.
              Cos Vincent was my hero.
              And then he went off me
              When Ty came along.
              So I…so I wrote this graffiti and it…well you know.
              You were there.
              I think I've been making up for that all of my life.
              But I never told him.
              Never said sorry.

              Instead I've been this grown up guy, this fucking guy
              I don't even recognise when I look in the mirror.

A guy that sits in on meetings and intervenes and
pretends he can't remember.
A guy whose wife is lying on our bed, grieving for
our friend, and I can't hold her, can't cry with her,
Cos there's a locked door, and I'm sitting on the floor,
on the other side.
Tonight I held our son, and it felt like he's the only
decent thing I've ever done.
The only true thing.
He looks like you Pamela. Like you used to, before
I…tired you out.
And he isn't this perfect, distant thing today.
He's just a tiny wee person.
Helpless.
A wish we once made.

Oh.
God.
When they carried him away
All you could see was
Blood.

Michael cries.

The door opens.

Michael and Pamela hold each other.

Arlene   I was pretending to sleep with my head on a rucksack,
on a floor in a station, when it came to me; that this
pain in my chest is a real thing, like a headache or rip
in my skin. It's love. And it's loss. And it's me.
Nothing I can run from, nothing I'll discover in a
youth hostel in India or Prague. So I got up. And
came back. To catch my boy. Everything was crystal
clear at last. I belong here. Loving you. With all the
pain in my heart.

Vincent	You sound…different.
Arlene	I am different. Because for the first time ever, I'm not scared. I'm not the terrified wifey, convinced she's an unfit mother with no words for her husband. I'm a woman. A woman who loves. And that means that whatever I do, as long as it comes from love, will be true. Just don't be scared. Hear me Vincent? Don't be scared. Hear me?
Vincent	I hear you.
Arlene	Cos your Gran's here to catch you now.
Vincent	Yeah. You caught me. And that's…something innit. Another chance eh? And we should use it.
Arlene	That's right. Use it to grieve for Ty.
Vincent	No. I can't. Not until I kill the plan.
Arlene	But what if people don't want to kill the plan? And how do you kill a plan? And what if they blame you for…
Vincent	We kill the plan. It's the plan that has to die. Nothing else. Then we grieve. Then we cry. No-one is allowed to cry until…

Vincent cries.

Arlene	No. You're right. We *can* do it. We're not scared anymore are we? We'll tell the world about the plan. I lost Grace and didn't say a word. Well now I'd like to see them shut me up. I'll shout from the rooftops and paint it on walls. We'll get megaphones and placards. And I'll handle everything so don't be scared. Anyway, anyone who prefers a computer to a megaphone deserves all they get.

Michael	Alright. The back door…
Vincent	Alright? No I'm not alright.
Arlene	I asked Michael to come round. Here, maybe he can help us. Get us the keys to the megaphone cupboard?
Michael	Anything.
Vincent	We don't need his help. He's the enemy. Tell him to fuck off.
Michael	What?
Vincent	I'll tell you what. You and your little Common Good Committee murdered Ty that's what.
Michael	Eh?
Vincent	You gave him the job, you gave him the gun and I'll bet you any money you set him up.
Michael	Don't be ridiculous.
Vincent	He told me!
Michael	You think the committee had Ty killed? That's…insane.
Vincent	Yeah right. The only reason he was there in the first place was to give folk the fear. Only that wasn't enough. Was it? But we're scared now. Oh aye. We're really scared now. And that's a coincidence is it? Ty was killed for your plan.
Michael	My plan? Your plan you mean.
Vincent	Eh?

Michael	It was your plan. It's never been my plan. It's always been about you. About you feeling superior to the rest of us suckers, blaming us all for your failure. And you're *still* doing it. My fault? It's your fucking fault.
Vincent	You killed him.
Michael	Oh fuck off. I'm fucking sick of this. I've done nothing but try to help you man. But you're never gonna stop looking down your nose at me. "You're not an artist", "You don't understand", "You don't do anything important". Well guess what, you're not an artist either. Never were. This isn't art, it's vandalism. And it's time to take fucking responsibility. You don't think I do anything important? Fucking watch me.
Vincent	Aye, on you go. Go back to the committee and cover it up. Cover up the murder! Get your youth centre and the rest of that money. That's not important. You'll never do anything important!
Arlene	Son…
Vincent	Naw. Forget him Gran. He's gone. It's just

> you and me.
> You and me.
> On every street corner
> With whistling
> megaphones.

Vincent & Arlene
> Say no to the Network!

> Vincent
> Pestering folk with
> petitions that never get
> signed.

                              The network's a con to make the
                              town worse.

Arlene   When you're powerless and lonely don't come crying
              to us.

                         Vincent
                              Even on the radio.
                   >: *Yes, that's right, I invented the whole thing. As*
              art yes. I know it does seem an unusual claim but…
                              No-one would tune in.
                              We were pathetic in the
                              face of Sweeny's
                              revolution, and talk of

Sweeny   The future. At our fingertips. Communication

Vincent   Needs people. Face to face not

Sweeny   Limited and medieval. Why should we reject what the
              rest of the world has embraced and

Vincent   Been imprisoned by. It's not a forward step it's

Sweeny   For the best. Of course it is, and the man on the street
              is

Vincent   A fucking idiot

Sweeny   Firmly behind it. Put this down to

Vincent   Greed

Sweeny   Grief. I believe he was a friend of the deceased.

Michael   I want in.

Sweeny	I thought you'd be on the corner with your alcoholic friend and his mad old mother.
Michael	She's his Gran. And he's not my friend. Sometimes I wonder if he's ever been my friend.
Sweeny	Well...there's not much left to do. Norman's covered most of the angles.
Michael	Where is your wee Rottweiler by the way?
Sweeny	He's been called away. On holiday.
Michael	There must be something. I need to prove that I've got something important in me. Please Sweeny. I need to prove someone wrong.
Sweeny	Well. Maybe there is a little thing. Mrs Young is being a bit tricky in the cheque dispensing department these days. Perhaps you could have a word and convince her that our way is the only way.
Michael	Okay. And listen, I reckon I can get us a deal on the PCs through the council.
Sweeny	Really?
Michael	Yeah. Leave all that to me.
Sweeny	Get the cheques and then we'll see.
Michael	Great. Look...the committee didn't have anything to do with...
Sweeny	Anything. The committee didn't have anything to do with anything. Goodbye Michael.

Norman   What do you think?

Sweeny   I think he could be useful.

>   Michael
>   Mrs Young? It's me.
>   Are you in here?
>   What…what is this?
>
>   Mrs Young
>   This is how I live
>   Michael.
>
>   Michael
>   I thought you…I
>   assumed… Where is
>   everything?
>   Where's your furniture?
>   Where's…?
>
>   Mrs Young
>   I don't have anything. I
>   used to.
>   But…it all went away.
>
>   Michael
>   What do you mean?
>   How could it go away?
>
>   Mrs Young
>   Stuff goes away.
>
>   Michael
>   Are you okay?
>
>   Mrs Young
>   Well there was no need
>   for it really. No-one

visited. I ate between
meetings and drank my
tea from foam cups in
corridors.
I haven't watched TV
since it turned real. I
have my clothes and a
bed and a picture of the
Queen.

Michael
But what have you been
doing?

Mrs Young
Nothing.

Michael
Nothing?

Mrs Young
Nothing. Absolutely
nothing. I tried to get
along. Tried to join in
and live well, but
nothing came my way.
I'd do what everyone
else seemed to do, and
I'd pray, but no. It
wasn't to be, for me.   I
was trapped. So I
stopped. I shut the
door and drew the
curtains and now I'm
just eating and just
drinking and just
sleeping. Just turning
invisible. And one day

I'll just vanish and
that'll be that. Oh here
listen to me havering
on. No-one comes here
you see, so my mouth's
moving to show off.
Silly old woman.   But I
assume you're from
Sweeny. Wanting me to
sign cheques. Well I
told him, I don't exist
now so how can I have
a signature? So. You
should go.

Michael

I don't want to go.

Mrs Young

Ach. That's nice. But
you don't know how I
feel.

Michael

I do. I really do.
But I also think there's
a way out. A way to
prove that our hearts
are still beating. And
for that I need two
things.

Mrs Young

What?

Michael

I need you to sign a
cheque for me.

Mrs Young
And?

Michael
I need you to come
back to my house for
tea. And maybe, stay
there for a while and
help us look after the
baby. We'd love that.
I'd love that.

Mrs Young
Would…what's your
baby's name?

Michael
Ty.

Vincent   And here we are.
The whole town, crowded round the monument, all
recently scrubbed.
For the big switch on
For the birth of Network Flood.
Wires in tubes underfoot, for the computers and the
screens, for the cameras and the microphones
As the world looks on.
Sweeny takes to the platform.
Taller than before.
Surrounded on all sides by New Flood.
As was.

Michael	Arlene. Vincent.
Vincent	Alright?
Michael	You're here. I didn't think you'd come.
Vincent	It's my plan after all.
Michael	Good. I wanted you to see this.
Arlene	We're still going to fight. We're not scared.
Michael	There's nothing to be scared of.
Vincent	Tell that to Ty.
Michael	I loved him too you know.
Vincent	Yeah. Well.

Michael	Vincent. Come and watch this with me.
Vincent	What so you can prove that you created something? That you're important?
Michael	No I just want you to see.
Vincent	I can see clearly mate don't worry. And I'll be watching every detail.
Michael	If we stand on your bench we'll get a better view.
Vincent	A better view of what? The life force of a town getting switched off, 2000 computers getting switched on?
Michael	I thought you hated this place?

Vincent	I used to sit here and imagine megaton bombs dropping from the sky. One on my house, one on this bench, one on the flats. My whole past gone.
Michael	But not now eh?
Vincent	No. Not now. Fuck knows what happened.
Michael	I know. You didn't mean it did you? Not really. That you blame me. For Ty.
Vincent	It's got to be someone's fault.
Michael	No. It doesn't. Some things just happen.
Vincent	I cannae handle that but.
Michael	Yes you can mate. Everybody can. It's amazing really, that people can always survive, always imagining that one day they'll be released. That's what they're all doing here today by the way. They're hopeful. We all are. You know, that's what I loved about your art Vincent. The letters. Cos they were always so hopeful. And real. You could hold them in your hands and feel it. When you found one, on a bench or that, it made you feel that magic can happen sometimes.

Sweeny	People of Network Flood. People of the world. The moment has arrived. Watch, as we switch on. Switch on the future. Switch off the past Ready?

103

Norman
Ready.

Sweeny   Join with me as I make a wish.

Vincent   There's a silence.
Like when someone is blowing a balloon beyond its
natural size.
Faces screw up. Breathing stops. Waiting for the pop.
I can see everyone exactly as they are.
And I can see myself.
In context at last. Me and him.
Did I know then?
Or did I find out later?
I can't remember.
But there's a connection as he smiles at me
Over the crowd and the glare I catch his eye
And it feels like we're from exactly the same place.
Born in the moment a women slipped and fell.
This has something to do with Grace.
I recognise the twist in his face from the mirror.
And yes, there's a horrible connection.
As he waves
And presses
The button.

bee   bee
    boo   boo

      cccccccccccccccccccccccccchhhhhhhhhhhhhhhhhhhhhhhhhhhhhhh

                        eeeeeeeeeeeeeeeeee
                  oo   oo
            oooooooooo   ooooo kct   kct
      eooo
      kh
   cchhh
  cccc
KKkc
>:...

                              Norman
                                 Aw shit.

                              Sweeny
                                 What? What is it?

>.........cccccccccchhhh ....   sh
                                           sh
                                           sh
                                           sh
                                           sh

                              Norman
                                 Shit

                              Sweeny
                                 What's happening?

Vincent   What's happening?

                              Sweeny
                                 What the hell is…?

105

>:................ a

TOOM

TA

TOOM

.
.
.
.
.
.
.
.
.
.
.
.
.
.
.
.
.
.
.
.
.
.
.
.

>: If destroyed true. If not destroyed true.

.
.
.
.
.
.
.
.
.
.
.

Vincent   What? What the fuck happened? Is everyone alright?

Arlene	I think so.
Vincent	The computers. The…ha. Ha ha ha! The computers. Of course. You see. They're machines. Just machines, not fucking…Gods. Machines break…
Michael	And explode…
Vincent	Even I forgot. I forgot that the thing with machines is, sometimes they just do not work.
Michael	Yeah. Especially if you buy them from Lightning Rod.
Vincent	Eh? Lightning…?
Michael	2000 PCs. Made the wee prick's day I can tell you. He'll be in Florida as we speak.
Vincent	You bought 2000 PCs from Lightning Rod? So you knew…?
Michael	Well, I asked him to be vigilant you know. Just to be sure.

Vincent smiles.

Vincent	Somewhere, Sweeny is coughing away burnt electric smoke Grinning for the cameras and trying to surf the joke. But he can't keep the hatred from his grin. And that joke was thin to begin with. There will be hard questions to answer from the sponsors And snide reports in the national papers. Later on. But now it's just that same old disappointment In everyone. The whole town.

And it strikes me,
Who are we to go against the majority?
They wanted this. Didn't they?
Maybe it would have given us hope in the short term.
If nothing else.
So were we wrong to fight against it?
But it's too late now,
Soon there's nothing left of the crowd just us.
Surrounded on all sides by the town of New Flood
As was.
Like a balloon that's burst.
But if you listen, you can still hear a pulse.

toom   ta toom   ta toom   ta toom   ta toom   ta toom   ta toom

Vincent   When Sweeny realised that Norman was gone and on
            the run
            He tried to pin the disaster with the computers on
            Michael.
            But to everyone's surprise, that one particular invoice
            was in Sweeny's name.
            Michael swore ignorance, and Mrs Young did the
            same.

            There was talk of mismanagement of course, but the
            fingers didn't really know where to point.
            Sweeny hinted to the police that Norman had drug and
            gun connections and was a big help to the
            investigation that brought him in and put him away.
            He never, at any point, mentioned me.

            He was offered a mercurial PR job in the city,
            With a nameless communications company who saw
            in him "the future".
            He burnt his files, washed his briefcase and left at
            three in the morning for The Dapper Life.
            He was happy.

Arlene felt that her first foray into protestation had been a marvellous success.

It had boosted her strength and confirmed her courage.

She was addicted now to the megaphone and adored the sound her voice made when it screeched in high pitch from the middle of a marching crowd.

She was plugged in. She was active. She was political.

From then on she was on every list, chained to every fence, last to stand at the sit down protest.

She wasn't scared. She knew what to do.

Mrs Young moved in with Michael and Pamela and was a big help.

She was a natural with baby Ty

And found that pushing him around town attracted strangers who wanted to drop a pound in the pram, and sometimes linger, to talk and be friends.

They assumed she was the Gran and she didn't put them right.

But more than that.

She saw in Ty a perfect mixture of all the good in Michael and Pamela.

She told them so daily.

And soon they saw it too.

Michael became the spokesman for the committee.

He regretted things publicly but reminded the dregs of uninterested reporters that some of the money remained.

Not enough for renewal, but enough for art, let's say.

In fact, he had an artist in mind.

It would be a public piece that the whole town could take part in.

It would give each individual hope and magic.

And with any luck give the artist a profile, a career.
It might just get him out of here.

I won't say the project was a memorial.
But I spent a lot of those days weeping and caressing
photographs.
But I didn't shed a single tear at the funeral.
Nothing in this, this art, reminds me of Ty and that's
good.
This is something new, something he'd be impressed
by.
Something true.

Michael   Well. All the money's gone. Pissed away.

Vincent   Oh thanks.

Michael   You know what though. I reckon this'll actually do
             the trick. It will actually make New Flood a better
             place. Even if only for a minute. Mark my words.
             Can you remember what your wish was? At school
             when we did this first. The one that was too heavy?

Vincent   I wished that I could make someone really happy.

Michael   That's a good one.

Vincent   Yeah.

Michael   You'll miss it.

Vincent   You know what, I think I will.

Michael   I mean, you'll miss the launch.

Vincent   I'll see it from the train.

Michael	Doesn't seem right, after all this, you leaving. You're coming back aren't you?
Vincent	Of course. This is my home.
Michael	And you've got the address I gave you, Pamela's brother, he's expecting you, he knows London so....
Vincent	I've got it.
Michael	Where's Arlene? Wouldn't think she'd miss this.
Vincent	She's where you should be. Down by the monument with the rest of the town. She doesn't do goodbyes anymore. They scare her. But she's right behind me.
Michael	Oh. Well. That's you. Well. Bye then.
Vincent	Thanks mate. Bye.
Michael	I'll miss you Vincent.
Vincent	I'll miss you too.

As the train pulls away from the unmanned station
It bends back on itself, rounding the base of a hill that doesn't have a name.
And for about a minute, the only view is of New Flood.
Normally the passengers look up, shiver and wonder about living here.
These streets. These houses.
They imagine a time in the future when they have to run away,
Perhaps from a terrible crime, or a terrible grief,
And need to be somewhere where they can't be found.
Would they come here?
No.

Normally, they feel the chill of the place on their skin,
like dust, for a second or two,
But shake it off, turning away from the window, back
to their books and magazines.
Normally.

But not today.
Because today when they look up they see something
unforgettable.

They see magic.
They see hope.
They see the result of the committee's spending and
my masterpiece.
They see something that makes them really happy.

They see a sky filled with ten thousand balloons.

Inside each balloon is a wish.
A secret wish, that each and every person in the town
has scrawled on tissue, Then folded and refused to tell.

I'm smiling.
Not at the sight of a thousand balloons,
But because I know,
And you do too,
That some of those wishes are bound to come true.

The train gathers speed.
Turning inland, moving on.
I see my face, reflected in the window
I'm there for a second,
Then gone.

The End

Sweeny got his big idea by misreading the following books/articles...

Classic Disputes in Sociology	P J Anderson
The Gutenberg Elegies	Sven Birkerts
Online essays	Mark Leyner
Being a Man: A Guide to New Masculinity	Mathew McKay
Bowling Alone	Robert D Putnam
Habits of the High-Tech Heart	Quentin J Schultze
War Of The Worlds	Mark Slouka

I would like to thank the EIF, all the Fellows and staff of The Institute of Advance Studies in Humanity Edinburgh University 2003, John Tiffany, Paines Plough, Dundee Rep and Kevin Donnelly who came up with the idea in the first place.

The play is for Caroline, with indestructible love.

IDT INDT